Rescuing Ruby

How I Rescued My Father from Greedy Cousins,
Thieving Attorneys
and The Florida Guardianship System

by

Robin Cohen Westmiller, J.D.

ISBN-13: 978-1463541927
ISBN-10: 1463541929

Introduction

The mounting problem with guardianship and conservatorship is not new for those who have been victimized. Yet it is only recently, with the media's attention on the Terri Schiavo case in 2005, that the financial and emotional abuse of our most vulnerable citizens has gained nationwide attention.

Articles have been written in publications including *AARP* magazine's "Stolen Lives" and published on Internet web sites such as "Justice For Florida Seniors," which is designed to "prevent guardianship abuse through education and action". A four-part series in the *Los Angeles Times* became the impetus for California Assembly Bill 1363: Omnibus Conservatorship and Guardianship Reform Act of 2006.

A March 22, 2006, episode of the television show *Boston Legal* featured a segment where a court-appointed guardian was stealing from his ward. When the judge continued the case, the guardian told the attorney he would find his own attorney who would charge him $500 an hour and the money would come from the estate of the ward. This part of the story line is, in many cases, true. (Hiring two thugs to beat up the guardian and force him to sign the release of his guardianship, however, was fiction.)

There are hundreds of horror stories of seniors who have been victimized from Florida to New York to California, but there have been no happy endings. Until now.

Magazine articles, media coverage, and even new legislation are totally ineffective when the controlling forces of attorneys and judges dictate an individual's rights to their own liberty and property. In many cases, the laws are as blind to the due process clause of the 14th amendment as the Statue of Justice is to the plight of the victims and their families. It takes extraordinary efforts of everyday heroes to help Lady Justice see, take notice, and act.

My mother always proclaimed the warning not to give your child the name of a bird because she'll spread her wings and fly away. What she should have said was not to name your child after an action hero, because she will have a life-long propensity towards fighting for truth and justice. Notwithstanding the more derogatory inferences to "round Robin" and "Rockin' Robin," such is my curse at having been named Robin. As a result, my aspirations were much more of the heroic breed of Robin Hood and Batman's partner.

My history of fighting injustices took me into the political arena in Glendale, California, in 1987 when the city's redevelopment agency was forcing small business owners from their property through the power of eminent domain. In 1988, I began a redistricting petition so that every resident, rich and poor, would have equal representation on the city council.

This compulsion led me to run for the Thousand Oaks, Conejo Valley Board of Education in 1994 to oppose a religious group's attempt to circulate abstinence materials in our public schools, which resulted in forcing the school board to remove the brochures from the schools. When I reviewed my daughter's history textbooks, I worked with the Jewish Anti-Defamation League to remove the anti-Semitic texts from the high school. With no committee or any funds, I single-handedly defeated an overblown 100 million dollar school bond initiative—twice.

I accomplished these heroic feats while raising three daughters, running a retail store with my husband, and publishing two romance novels under my pen name of Raven West.

A mid-life crisis soon after my 50th birthday led me to enroll in the Southern California Institute of Law, where I hoped to find a way to continue my education in an area that I felt would afford me the opportunity to continue my pursuit of justice in a more lucrative career. (Super heroes rarely receive compensation for their endeavors.)

Yet, with all my experience fighting against the injustices of society, I was unaware of the true evil that was brewing within my very own family—an evil so insidious that it eventually cost my parents their home, their life savings, and nearly their lives.

They say truth is stranger than fiction. As a writer of fiction, I can verify the truth of that platitude because in my wildest imagination I could not have possibly created the story that became my own reality horror show. The list of villains and their accomplices rivals any comic book character's nemesis. The battle was waged in a court of law and won by a daughter whose love for her father was stronger than steel.

This is the true story of my incredible fight to rescue my father from the clutches of financial vampires comprised of my cousins, the attorneys Howard Raab and G. Mark Shalloway, the guardian Lee Eakin, and Neil Newstein of

Ferd & Gladys Alpert Jewish Family and Children's Services of West Palm Beach, Florida.

Our family owes a huge debt of gratitude to Elder Law Attorney Sheri L. Hazeline, an intelligent young woman who went up against a powerful law firm and beat them at their own game. If not for her advice and support, I am certain my father would be living in a Medicaid facility in Florida and all of our family's assets would have transferred into the bank accounts of Shalloway & Shalloway and the trust fund of Jewish Family Services.

Rescuing Ruby is not only an interesting and informative account of how our family was able to defeat the Florida guardianship system, but will serve to help other families who feel helpless against a heartless probate court system. This book will alert our baby-boomer generation to the early signs of financial abuse and undue influence by relatives and caregivers and offer ways to protect their loved ones from the predators who use the legal process for their own gains.

It is my hope that our story will offer help and support to those who have been victimized so that no other family has to suffer the loss of their elderly parents, and all they've worked their entire lives to accumulate, to some nameless, heartless agency and its attorneys.

My ultimate goal in writing this book is to expose the insidious web of legalized theft perpetuated by judges and attorneys and the national tragedy of a corrupt guardianship system.

If this tragedy can happen to someone as well known and loved as Ruby Cohen of Cohen's Bakery in Ellenville, New York, it can happen to anyone.

The work of an action hero is never finished until evil is exposed and eradicated once and for all.

Chapter 1

My father, Ruby Cohen, owned and operated Cohen's Quality Bakery in Ellenville, New York, his entire adult life. During the '50s and '60s, the Catskills was *the* summer vacation destination for many Jewish families. No visit to Ellenville was complete without a stop in Cohen's Bakery, home of the "World Famous Raisin Pumpernickel." Everyone knew Ruby Cohen. He was as famous as any actor or politician and was regarded with respect and admiration by everyone who met him.

Dad was a charter member of the Ellenville Elks Lodge #1971 and was an active member for over fifty years. He was the founding president of the Ellenville Lions Club and was honored as "Citizen of the Year" in 1997. He was a wonderful husband, a great father, and a loving and kind grandfather to my three daughters: Tandy, Kimberly and Michelle.

Ruby was a man anyone would have been proud to call their father, so much so that when my cousins' father passed away in 1968, "Uncle" Ruby assumed the role of their surrogate father. Their relationship became a constant tug-of-war that raged on throughout my adulthood, and increased after my two cousins, Beverly and Diane, moved to Los Angeles in 1984. Even though I knew we would never be the perfect extended family, never in my wildest imagination did I suspect they would conspire with other cousins to steal my father's entire life savings and try to separate him permanently from my mother.

I was working as an assistant editor at *Healthy Living Magazine* in Southern California in the spring of 2002 when I

received a phone call from my mother informing me that my
father had suffered a minor stroke while working at the
bakery. I asked her if she needed me to go to New York, but
she told me she was handling things and that Dad was fine.
The stroke did little damage to his ability to function
physically; but his memory and mental faculties were
severely impaired, although at the time, none of us knew the
extent of the injury, or what his demented state would
eventually cost our family.

   The stroke forced Dad to sell our family business.
After over eighty years, "Cohen's Bakery" would no longer
be owned by a Cohen. In May of 2003, I traveled to
Ellenville to attend the New York State Elks Convention
with my dad. I could immediately see the effects the stroke
had on his ability to function in a normal fashion. Although
Mom was trying to maintain a positive attitude, I could tell
Dad's deteriorating health was taking a toll on her as well.

   Mom told me she had received phone calls from the
local police telling her Dad had been found wandering
through town and that she needed to pick him up. Believing
he still owned the bakery, he would stop in and occupy his
former office chair, and the police would have to be called to
drive him home. On more than one occasion, Dad stole the
car keys and drove off without telling anyone where he was
going. He usually ended up at the American Legion bar.

   I was amazed that my seventy-nine-year-old mother
was holding up as well as she appeared to be. Having
volunteered for years with the Ellenville First Aid and
Rescue Squad, she had knowledge of basic first aid and knew
all the emergency personnel at the local hospital by name.
Mom's ability to take care of my dad in his condition was
truly amazing.

In November 2003, my three daughters and I flew to New York to celebrate Thanksgiving with my parents. Dad was his usual jovial self but complained that he felt like a prisoner because my mother was doing her best to ensure that Dad followed his doctor's orders of not driving or drinking alcohol.

In spite of what the doctor had told him, Dad insisted on having a few shots of scotch and eating the pumpkin pie dessert. After dinner, he became dizzy and passed out in the bathroom. We rushed him to the hospital with dangerously high blood pressure and blood sugar levels. Fortunately, the doctors were able to stabilize his vitals and we brought him home that night. Dad insisted he had the flu, that he'd soon be back to "normal" and would be able to fly out to California to attend Michelle's high school graduation in June. Although we all hoped she was wrong, my mother said there was no way he would be able to make the trip in his condition.

When I phoned my mother a few weeks later, she told me she was concerned because Dad was receiving a number of phone calls from my cousin Gail Lerner, who lived in Florida. Gail had never been very close to our family. There had always been animosity between Gail and my mother, although I had never understood or knew the reasons why. Mom said she had tried to tell Gail that Dad wasn't strong enough to travel alone and that he wouldn't be able to visit her as he had in the past. Mom said she'd also tried to explain that Dad was having problems with his memory, sometimes forgetting to take his medication, and, worse, forgetting where the bathroom was when he needed to use it. Mom said Gail argued with her, insisting that Mom was exaggerating and that "Uncle Ruby" wanted to go to Florida. Mom's warnings to Gail caused their old friction to flare up again and their conversations became increasingly hostile. This caused my mother to become intensely upset, and she eventually stopped talking to Gail.

On a chilly end-of-winter day in March 2004, I received a frantic phone call from my mother. Dad had packed a suitcase and said he was going to Florida. Normally, this wasn't an unusual occurrence. Dad would often vacation for a few weeks in a warmer climate with his family, while Mom stayed home with her friends and social engagements. However, unlike previous vacations, Dad's health was now a major issue. Mom was very concerned about his plans to have someone drive him to the airport in Newburgh, his ability to change planes in Atlanta, and arrive safely in Fort Lauderdale. I spoke to Dad and maybe it was a daughter's unrealistic denial of reality, but I believed him when he told me that he was fine and not to worry.

I asked Dad if he would be staying with Gail in Florida, but he didn't confirm or deny where he would be staying. He told me that he was only going to be gone for a few weeks until the weather warmed up back home, and that he'd be back in New York in time for the 2004 New York State Elks Convention in May, which I had planned on attending with him.

In spite of my mother's best efforts to talk sense into my father, Dad phoned a friend to drive him to the airport and headed out the door. Although Mom was desperate about not wanting him to leave, there wasn't anything a ninety-five pound, seventy-nine-year-old woman could physically do to stop him. We could not have possibly imagined that this one "small step" Dad took that day would alter the course of the lives of my family forever, plunging all of us into a two-year-long nightmare.

A few days after Dad arrived in Florida, I called Gail to see how things were going and to talk to Dad. Gail told me he was out to lunch with friends and would call me when he returned. Three days later with no returned phone call from Dad, I called again. This time Gail told me he was resting, but that she would have him call me as soon as he was awake. I didn't receive a phone call from Dad this time either, but with the three-hour time difference between California and New York, I didn't think anything was unusual at first about not being able to catch him at a convenient time.

My concerns began when my daughter Tandy called from Oklahoma and told me that she had been unable to speak to her grandfather either. Tandy said that whenever she called, Gail would always say that Dad was either sleeping or out with friends. Tandy's messages for him to return her calls went unanswered...and Tulsa had only a one-hour time difference from Florida.

March 19, 2004, nine days after Dad had left New York, I received an email from Gail. Suddenly, it seemed Dad's visit to Florida was turning into something much longer than a two-week vacation. I had no idea who Henry and Sheri Solomon were, or what a geriatric care manager was, or why my father would be looking for an apartment in Florida when, as far as I knew, he was planning on returning to Ellenville.

I emailed a reply and tried to call her, but the call went directly to Gail's voice mail. I left several messages trying to get in touch with my father and get some clarification as to what was going on, but never received a reply. Meanwhile, my mother was alone in New York, unable to eat, losing weight, and literally worried sick about where her husband was.

I kept trying to call but no one would answer. Finally, about a week later, by some miracle, my father answered the phone. I asked him about the email and the apartment and what his plans were. His voice was so cold and distant as he said, "I'm leaving New York and never going back."

I couldn't believe what I was hearing. This didn't sound like my dad. I felt the muscles in my stomach tighten, the first subconscious warning signs of the dangers to come.

"What are you talking about?" I said, "Did you tell Mom?"

"I haven't talked to your mother. She hasn't called me since I got here. All she cares about is the money. Don't call me anymore."

Then, the phone went dead.

I immediately hit the speed redial button, but no one answered. My next call was to my mother. Mom was crying so hysterically she could barely speak into the phone.

"The bank just called. Your father tried to cash a check for $50,000!"

"You're kidding!" I replied. "Do you have that much in your checking account?"

"Of course not! He knows that. The amount was crossed out and the correction wasn't initialed. I don't think the handwriting on the date is his. Your father needs to come home. He doesn't know what he's doing."

I should have immediately left my job, quit law school, and been on the next plane to Florida. But since I'd already made plans to go to New York in May, I didn't think there was any reason to change my plans and leave earlier. Mom told me she had closed out all of their joint accounts, and had put everything in her name to protect herself from future surprises. She sounded as though she were handling the situation quite well.

We both expected Dad would be coming back to Ellenville, but we found out that my cousin had other plans.

A few days later, my mother faxed me a copy of one of my father's IRA accounts, which notified us that the beneficiaries had been changed from my three daughters to my four cousins: Beverly Cohen Scotti, Diane Cohen, Roberta Grundt, and Gail Lerner. It was obvious that my cousins knew about this change in beneficiaries, in spite of their claims not to have known what Gail was doing. There wasn't any way Gail could have filled in the exact month, day, and year of their births unless she had contacted them for the information. According to our financial advisor, this change in beneficiaries should have never taken place without my mother's signature; and obviously, my mother never agreed to nor signed such a change.

I was furious. I knew my father would never take money from his only grandchildren, especially with Michelle, the youngest, graduating high school that year. Over the years, Dad had made many investments for his granddaughters' education. Even though they never asked for or expected financial support, their relationship with their grandfather was tantamount throughout their lives. Both my parents had attended all the special occasions from the day they were born. Each of their Bat Mitzvahs, Tandy and

Kimberly's high school graduations, and our yearly visits to New York were the highlights of my father's life. I knew there was no way he would have cut them out of any financial support, and definitely would not have given it to his adult nieces. Someone was manipulating him, and I knew exactly who that was. Unfortunately, I had no idea at the time what lengths Gail was willing to go to keep my father from his family, until I received another frantic phone call from my mother.

Mom had received a notice that her power of attorney was revoked. It was signed by my father and witnessed by my cousin and someone by the name of Frank, who I later learned was Gail's boyfriend. The form was dated April 14, 2004. In just over one month, Gail had managed to find an attorney and gain control over my father and his entire estate. The paper listed Dad's new address. I looked the address up on the Internet and discovered that the location was the Newport Place Retirement Home in Boynton Beach. I immediately phoned the facility and asked to speak to Ruby Cohen. The receptionist told me that Mr. Cohen was not to receive any phone calls, by order of his power of attorney. I told the woman that I was his daughter and I wanted to speak to my father, but she refused to connect my call.

I called Mom and tried to reassure her that I would take care of everything. It was just an empty promise as I had absolutely no idea how or what I could do from three thousand miles away, especially since Gail now held my father's power of attorney and had full access to influence him to agree to do anything she told him to do. What was so heartbreaking to our family was that my daughters, who had always been so close to their grandfather, had lost all communication with him. I was helpless to do anything to rectify the situation.

Hoping to find some help, I phoned my cousin Beverly, who lived a few miles from me. She was very cold and said she didn't want to get involved since it didn't have anything to do with her. I then tried to contact my cousins Bob and Norman Feldner, sons of my father's late sister Jean, but they refused to listen to my cries for help. It became obvious to me that every one of my father's family was siding with Gail, for reasons I could not understand.

In the past, I had always invited my cousins to our family's events, but they would only attend when my father was visiting. I had held a graduation party in June of 2000 at my home for my daughter Tandy. Beverly and Diane took this opportunity to present Dad with a Father's Day present, right in front of my guests. This led to many uncomfortable questions.

Whenever my parents came to California, my cousins would invite my father to visit them in Palm Springs, party on their yacht, attend their children's weddings, and attend many charity events. My mother and I were never included in their invitations. When Beverly was married, I suggested that she ask Dad to walk her down the aisle. She thought it was a wonderful idea, and he agreed. Neither my mother nor I were invited to the wedding. Beverly said it was a "small family wedding."

Although I wasn't surprised that Beverly had responded the way she did when I called her for help, I never expected that all of my cousins would conspire to such incredible lengths to try to take my father away from my mother and me, and, worse, his grandchildren. However, they never expected the lengths I would go to in order to prevent them from succeeding.

The gauntlet had been thrown, the battle had begun, and it was going to be a long and bloody war before it was over. With no siblings, no other family members on my side, my mother in New York, and my father in Florida, I was facing my very own Bermuda Triangle. And I was facing it "relatively" alone.

Chapter 2

Five-thirty in the morning is never a good time for the telephone to ring. Five-thirty on a Monday morning the week of law school final exams is the worst possible time to be awakened by a ringing phone. I'd been studying all night and was barely awake when I picked up the receiver, but I was instantly wide-awake when I heard Mom sobbing so hard she could hardly get the words out.

"Your father filed for divorce! I was served with the papers this morning. I don't know what I'm going to do!"

I half hoped that I was still asleep and that the phone call was only a nightmare; I would wake up soon and find out that Dad was still in New York with everything back to normal. However, that slim hope was dashed by the sound of my mother crying through the telephone. I was filled with an all-too-real anger. Whatever Gail's intentions were, my immediate concerns were with Mom.

Having grown up the Depression era of the '20s and '30s, my mother's family had been nearly impoverished. My mother was the youngest of three children and two stepchildren. Her mother had died when she was a baby, and her father had remarried so that the state welfare agency would not take away his children. My grandfather did his best to support his wife and five children, but times were very difficult. Money and food had been in short supply.

My parents married in the early fifties and both worked very hard to make the family business, Cohen's Bakery, a success. Believing that my father could have "married better," his family never accepted Mom as a suitable wife and they never failed to remind him of this fact. It caused a huge division in our family. As hard as my mom worked to create a loving home for my father and me, the influence of my dad's family and their continuous criticism of his life created a rift between my parents that only grew larger throughout the years. Now these rifts threatened the very existence of our family unit and threatened to destroy my mother on every level: physically, emotionally, and especially financially.

There was no choice but for my mother to hire an attorney. Since my parents lived in a small town, most of the attorneys there knew, or had represented, my father in some manner. This created a legal conflict for my mother in her attempt to find an attorney to represent her in a divorce action. Mom's future looked as if her worst nightmare was about to come true. She was terrified of losing her home, all of her life's savings, and returning to a life of poverty. I tried to assure her that this was not going to happen, but her childhood memories and fears proved difficult to overcome.

Somehow, I managed to get through exam week and passed all three of my law school courses: Criminal Law, Torts, and Contracts, none of which covered the complexities of New York divorce laws. At the time, I was working for a family law firm in Thousand Oaks, California, but they were of little help to me because of the vast differences between California and New York laws. The best I could do for Mom was to be on the next plane to New York. Since I had planned on attending the New York State Elks Convention that weekend anyway, I already had my plane ticket in hand for May 14. I never made the convention.

It is hard to explain the spectrum of emotions I felt when I walked into my parents' house the night of May 14.

What was supposed to have been a joyous visit attending the convention with my dad had turned into a funeral, without a body. Mom was sitting at the kitchen table, a location of many happy family celebrations, anniversaries, and birthdays. In my mind's eye, I could see my children sitting around that very table from the time they were infants in high chairs to the previous Thanksgiving only six months ago. It was more than I could stomach to see my mother in tears, staring at the papers that accused her of abandonment and abuse. Nevertheless, I had to be strong for her sake, even as I was falling apart emotionally.

After eating a five-course meal that Mom insisted on preparing, I began reading over the action for divorce. My first comment was that the signature on the complaint was not my father's signature. I've seen my father's signature on many documents and whoever signed these papers was either not my father, or if it was his signature, then Dad wasn't in a normal state of mind when he signed them. The accusations were ludicrous. I assured my mother that we'd contest all the allegations and the case would be dismissed for lack of cause. This would have been the procedure in California, but, unfortunately, we were not in California. I soon realized that it was going to take a lot more than a simple motion to dismiss to make the case go away, especially after I read Gail's affidavits attacking my mother, which were attached to the complaint.

Mom and I made an appointment with the one attorney in Ellenville who didn't know my father. He proceeded to go through the case, *after* mom paid him a hefty retainer. As we went through each item on the complaint, both my mother and I were in shock. Did my father really believe what he had signed? The papers incorrectly identified me as Susan Westmiller, accused my mother of depleting an account in an irrevocable family trust (which was legally impossible), and, among other accusations, his "sworn testimony" stated that he had been released from a New York City hospital after a triple by-pass operation in 1998 and had gone home by bus! Dad knew I had flown to New York and drove him home the day after the New York Yankees won the World Series...and I'm certainly no bus driver!

I knew my father would never believe these vicious lies, unless someone was influencing him; but without any way of contacting him, I was helpless—and I was angry! Even though I understood Dad's stroke had affected his capacity to reason and that he would never have accused me of such horrible acts under normal circumstances, I felt betrayed emotionally and deeply hurt. I felt as if he had not only filed for a divorce from my mother, but from me as well. My fifty-year-old adult self needed to be strong for my mother, but the child who had grown up in that house felt like a five-year-old whose daddy had left and was never coming home. I woke up many times throughout that night expecting to hear the garage door open and Dad coming home from work. The silence was deafening.

A few days later, I phoned my daughter Tandy who was living in Tulsa, Oklahoma, and attending the Spartan College of Aeronautics. I told her about the divorce action, and that I couldn't contact Dad because the people at the place where he was staying wouldn't let me talk to him. Tandy offered to fly to Florida and see him in person. She said that she could take a few days off from class and be in Ft. Lauderdale in a few hours. I thought that was a great idea and gave her the address of the Newport Beach Retirement Community. I asked her to call me as soon as she talked to Dad. I also gave her the phone number of a very good friend of mine, Vic D'Alessio, who I had kept in touch with since

high school. He lived in Sunrise, a few miles from the Fort
Lauderdale airport. I also called my Aunt Kay, my mother's
stepsister, and Uncle Phil Palent, who lived in Sunrise also,
and asked them if Tandy could stay with them for a few days
while she was in Florida. Uncle Phil immediately said "Of
course." (Mom's side of the family had always been
wonderful!)

I was confident that when my father saw his
granddaughter, she would be able to undue all the damage
my cousin had done, convince him to drop the divorce action,
and come home.

She almost didn't get the chance.

Chapter 3

With Tandy on her way to Florida to talk to Dad, I was able to relax a bit and spend some time with one of my closest friends from high school, Warren Garrison, who still lived in Ellenville. It was a welcome distraction to have someone to reminisce about the better times of our youth growing up in the heart of the Catskill Mountains. The trip down memory lane reminded me of how much a part of New York history my father and Cohen's Bakery had played in the lives of so many people in Ellenville and the many New Yorkers who had spent their summers escaping the heat of the city to vacation in "the mountains." With such a wonderful past and a lifetime spent living in New York, I knew there was no way my father would have left his life, his long-time friends, my mother, and his home had he been in a healthy state of mind. I was confident that once my daughter talked to him, Dad would be home soon.

When the phone rang, I was expecting good news. What I heard nearly stopped my heart.

"Mom, I'm at the address you gave me, and Grandpa's not here," Tandy said.

"Where is he?" I began to panic.

"They don't know. All they told me was that he'd fallen down and was taken to a hospital, but they won't tell me where."

I could tell by the sound of her voice that my daughter was in tears. She choked through the story. She had landed at the airport, rented a car, and had driven to the Newport Beach facility where we thought Dad was living, where she had discovered that not only was my father no longer at the facility, but no one there knew where he was or would tell her what had happened to him. They would only say that he had fallen down and had been taken to a hospital, but they were under instructions by his "power of attorney" not to release any information. Tandy had then called the local police department. An officer had met her at the office, but told her there was nothing they could do. The officer had given her a list of hospitals in the area and suggested she call them.

Tandy called Gail, who answered the phone but pretended that she wasn't Gail and that Gail wasn't home. When Gail finally admitted it was actually her on the phone, she told Tandy that my father did not want to see her.

I told my mother what was going on in Florida and that we had no idea where Dad was. My cousin Beverly, who lived in California, knew how close my daughters were to my Dad. In desperation, I called her thinking that she might be able to convince Gail to tell Tandy where her grandfather was so she could visit him.

When Beverly called back, I was expecting her to tell me what I needed to know. I shouldn't have been surprised when she backed up Gail's story, saying that she had spoken to my father and that he had told her he didn't want to see Tandy. I knew Beverly was lying and asked her to tell me what number she had called to talk to Dad so that I could give the phone number to Tandy. She flatly refused to divulge the information. It was obvious that my cousins would do whatever they could to keep my father away from our family.

My daughter frantically continued to phone the hospitals in Florida, but she couldn't find a Rubin Cohen in any of the hospitals that she called. Tandy only had one more day before she had to fly back to Oklahoma. I phoned the office of my father's attorney in Florida in the hope that at least his secretary would understand how desperate we were to locate my father, so that my daughter could see him, but neither she nor the attorney would help.

I'm not normally a religious person, but for some reason, at that moment I felt the need for spiritual guidance. I phoned my parents' temple in Ellenville to talk to their rabbi, thinking that perhaps he could persuade Gail to tell him where she had hidden my father. By lucky coincidence, Rabbi Frank happened to be in Florida visiting former Ellenville residents. I explained the situation to the secretary and gave her Tandy's cell phone number in the hope that our rabbi would be able to locate my father and relay the message to her. I also knew that Rabbi Frank would tell us the truth about my father's wishes regarding a visit from his granddaughter.

By luck, or by the grace of God, Rabbi Frank happened to be visiting with my father in the Bethesda Memorial Hospital in Boynton Beach when he received the message on his cell phone. Rabbi Frank called Tandy and then handed his phone to Dad. After three days of frantically searching for her grandfather, Tandy was finally able to talk to him directly. Because she had been told that he did not wish to see her, she was a bit hesitant at first. Not surprisingly, she found out that he had not been told that she was in Florida, or that she had been trying to find him. She asked him how he was doing and if she could come see him. His response was immediate. "Of course you can come see me!" he told her.

Tandy phoned me immediately with the address of the hospital. She said she was on her way to see him and would call me as soon as she could. I was so happy and relieved because the truth would finally come out and my father would soon be on his way home.

I knew in my heart that my father would never have normally said he didn't want to see Tandy, but with his state of mind and the mental poison that Gail had been feeding him, I didn't know what he would do when Tandy arrived. If he said he didn't wish to see Tandy, my daughter would be devastated, and I was two thousand miles away in New York, unable to help her. I sat staring at the phone for the next three hours. When Tandy finally had the opportunity to call me and tell me about her visit, I knew I had to get to Florida on the next available flight.

Tandy told me that when she had arrived at the hospital, the nurse couldn't give her any medical information because she was not listed as family. In fact, the only names on the list were Gail's and someone named "Cookie." Under HIPPA (Health Insurance Portability and Accountability Act) privacy laws, the staff couldn't divulge any information to anyone except family members and according to their records, the only family my father had was his niece, Gail Lerner, who was visiting Dad when Tandy arrived. It was obvious that Gail was doing everything she could to make sure no one knew my father had any other family except for her.

Tandy had spoken to Gail to find out what her grandfather's condition was and why he was in the hospital. Gail told her he was doing well and would be back in the retirement center in a month. It was all my daughter could do to hold her temper in check, but it was more important for her to see her grandfather than it was to start a fight with Gail.

Tandy's visit with Dad was wonderful. Although we had been told that he didn't want to see Tandy, he was actually ecstatic to see her. He didn't know exactly what had happened, but he mentioned that he had been bleeding and had to have several blood transfusions. He didn't know why his shoulder was in a sling, or why his foot hurt. Tandy said he was unable to get out of bed to get into the wheelchair and had to have two people help him get up. When she took him into the dining room, he couldn't remember if he had a TV in his room, although they had been watching it just minutes before. It was obvious that his mental state hadn't improved. In fact, it had become much worse since he had left New York, and it was hard for Tandy to maintain a normal composure. Tandy told me Dad hadn't wanted her to leave, and that it broke her heart to be able to spend only one hour with him, after being in Florida for four days, because of Gail's refusal to tell her where he was.

I knew I had to go to Florida and see Dad before Gail had the chance to move him again. I found Dad's Delta frequent flyer card in his desk drawer and used it to book a flight to Fort Lauderdale on Friday morning, May 21. Vic picked me up at the airport and drove me to the hospital that afternoon. When I arrived, I immediately went to the nurses' station to inquire about my father's condition. They told me, as they had told Tandy earlier, that they could not release any information except to family members but, if Dad recognized me as his daughter, they would add me to the list as next of kin.

When I found Dad's hospital room, the nurse asked him who I was and he said, without hesitation, "That's my

daughter!" There was a woman in the room with Dad when I
walked in. She told me her name was Sylvia Gardner and
claimed to be a cousin of my father. I had never heard of her
and curtly asked her to leave us alone so we could talk. She
gave me a dirty look but reluctantly left the room. I spoke to
Dad's attending physician and learned that he had suffered
another stroke while at the Newport Beach facility. Dad had
fallen down and shattered his shoulder, which was why it
was in a sling, and the pain in his foot was from a diabetic
ulcer, which had formed on his heel. In addition, he had total
kidney failure and needed to be on dialysis. Quite a different
story from the "he's fine and will be back at the retirement
home in a month" lie that Gail had told my daughter.

From our conversation, I learned that Dad believed
every lie Gail had told him. He accused my mother of trying
to steal all his money. He was convinced that I had no plans
for finishing law school. He said I had taken his car. I felt as
if I were talking to a stranger. I reminded him that he had
offered his car to Michelle since he couldn't buy her a new
one for graduation. I reminded him that my first year of law
school was over and I planned on taking the bar exam in
2007.

I had brought my parents' income tax refund check. It
was made out to both of them, and I explained that he needed
to endorse the check so my mother could cash it. The check
was going to be divided between him and my mother and
held in an escrow account by their attorneys until the divorce
was over. I tried explaining the details to Dad but he kept
forgetting the conversation. I wondered how he would have
known what he was signing, in his current state of mind,
especially his testimony on the divorce papers against my
mother and me.

Dad didn't remember falling down. He didn't remember how he was injured. He had no idea why he wasn't leaving with me. He kept asking me how Mom was and for me to tell her that he was doing well and not to worry. He was adamant that as soon as he was better, he was going home to New York. I didn't have the heart to tell him he wasn't going to get better and that his doctor had told me he would be on dialysis for the rest of his life. I explained that my mother was going into the hospital Wednesday for tests and I had to return to New York, but I'd be back in a few weeks to see him and find a way to bring him home.

At first, he didn't know what I was talking about when I mentioned the divorce. He assured me he would phone the attorney and have him cancel the proceedings. I should have handed him the phone the minute he said it, but I was so happy to see him it never occurred to me that five minutes after I left, Gail would be back to convince him to do just the opposite—and a great deal more.

The timing of events instigated by Gail was much too suspicious to have been a coincidence. Soon after Dad arrived in Florida on March 18, he supposedly had tried to cash a check for $50,000 and the very next day, Gail sent me an email saying everything was "fine." Shortly after, on April 2, Gail had taken my father to a divorce attorney. On April 14, she changed the names of the beneficiaries on Dad's American Fund IRA, the same day my mother's power of attorney was revoked. Gail moved Dad into the Newport facility in May without telling anyone in our family and while he was there, he "fell", shattered his shoulder and ended up in the hospital with total kidney failure and an ulcerated heel.

The worst part of this situation was that my father still believed Gail was "taking good care of him." In his demented state of mind, Dad had no recollection of any of the circumstances that were tearing our family apart. Gail had worked very fast to gain not only his trust, but his trust accounts as well.

It was up to me to work even faster to undue the damage she'd caused and to save my father from further deterioration of his health. I had no idea what I was going to do to stop her when she had total access to him and complete control over every aspect of his life.

I left Florida to fly back to New York on Sunday morning. The in-flight movie was *The Notebook*, a story about an elderly couple dealing with the devastation of memory loss.

I cried all the way home.

Chapter 4

After I returned to New York, I met with my mother's
attorney, Frank Eck. He immediately sent a letter to Dad's
Florida attorney, Howard Raab, along with a check for half
the tax refund, and took my statement on what had transpired
during my brief visit with my father. I asked Frank how it
was possible for my father to file any kind of legal action
when his mental and physical conditions were so precarious.
He didn't have an answer. However, he did question the fact
that Raab had notarized Dad's signatures; especially since
Gail had herself witnessed the revocation of the power of
attorney, and then had it reassigned to her immediately after.
This seemed to be a huge conflict of interest and a violation
of notary rules and procedures. I felt confident that Frank
would help put an end to the divorce action when I told him
my father was going to call Raab and tell him to dismiss the
case. Frank told me that he knew Howard Raab and was not
at all as confident as I was.

I stayed a few extra days in New York while Mom
had some tests taken in the Ellenville Hospital to try and find
out why she continued to lose weight and was starting to
have difficulty standing erect. All the tests came back
negative. Her doctor told her to eat more protein, exercise,
and watch her blood sugar.

Mom had never been in the hospital for more than a
day in her life. She had always been a very strong,
independent woman. I was concerned about her health, but
she assured me that she was fine. She said that Dad would be
home as soon as he was healthy enough to travel, and that I
shouldn't worry about her. She sounded so positive that I
believed her. Since she had many friends who were in

contact with me by telephone and email, I left for home thinking everything was going to be fine.

June was a very hectic month for me. My daughter Michelle was graduating from high school and both my other daughters, Kimberly and Tandy, were flying home from school to attend the ceremony. Because this was the first major family celebration since the birth of Tandy in 1982 that my parents did not attend, it was a bittersweet reunion. I could tell that my daughters were trying to maintain an optimistic attitude, but we were all feeling a huge absence because my mom and dad weren't with us. On the way to the school for the graduation ceremony, we called Dad. He had been transferred to the Boulevard Manor Nursing Home in Boynton Beach and didn't have a phone in his room, but the nurse brought Dad a cell phone so we could talk to him. We told him that we were on the way to Michelle's graduation and we missed him. It broke our hearts when he said, "When I get better, I'll be out there for the graduation. When is it?"

A few days later, I received a package from Howard Rabb that I thought would contain the divorce dismissal Dad told me he was going to request. Instead, to my horror, the package contained stacks of more legal motions, including Gail's affidavit stating that Mom and I had continued to take Dad's money. There was even a court-ordered injunction prohibiting my mother from withdrawing any further family assets, in effect freezing her access to any funds from which to pay her bills or to buy food. I couldn't believe what I was reading. I called the nursing home and asked to speak to my father. I heard the nurse tell Dad that I was on the phone. Then I heard Dad say, "I'm not talking to anyone. They're all out to get me!"

I was in shock. In spite of the fact that Dad hold told me he was going to stop the divorce proceedings, somehow Gail had managed to convince Dad to continue the action and to get Raab to go after my mother even more fiercely than before.

Meanwhile, I'd been receiving emails from my mother's friend, Sarah Klein, in Ellenville informing me that Mom's health was declining. She said Mom was having a difficult time sitting up and was starting to use a walker. I phoned Mom to see what was going on. She told me she was fine, but wanted to know who had come into her house and left a cake on the table. Evidently, she was starting to hallucinate and was not in any way, shape, or form "fine."

I phoned the Ellenville Hospital and asked to have a visiting nurse check up on Mom and let me know what was going on. Then I phoned my father in Florida, and this time he talked to me. I broke down crying on the phone. I told him that Mom was seriously ill, and begged him to call his attorney to end the divorce action. Dad told me not to cry. He said he would make the call; and, as a father should do, said he would take care of everything.

Nothing Dad promised me that day took place. A few days later another set of affidavits documents arrived from Raab's office. In these documents, my father supposedly testified, under oath, that my visit had upset him, that we had no relationship, and that he never wanted to see my mother again. The signature on the paper was in very shaky handwriting and didn't look like Dad's at all. Although he had signed the testimony under penalty of perjury, I seriously doubt he had any idea what he was signing. Thinking we might have evidence of fraud, I contacted a professional handwriting analyst to compare Dad's signatures.

It was obvious to me that my cousins, and the divorce attorney she had hired, were manipulating my father. With Dad in the nursing home, I had no idea who was paying the attorney fees. Since Gail had Dad's power of attorney, I surmised she was writing checks from the joint account that she had opened in both her and my father's name. With complete access to all of our family's investments, and complete control over my father's state of mind, Gail was close to stealing everything my parents had worked for their entire lives. Even worse, she was stealing my father from my mother and my children.

Phone calls and emails to my other cousins in California continued to go unanswered. Now when he really needed them, all the people who had professed their "love" for Uncle Ruby when he was the party man, and paying for the privilege, were nowhere to be found.

I tried calling several California lawyers from my contacts with the Ventura County Bar Association but they told me that they couldn't take my case because California attorneys do not have the legal authority to represent California clients in out-of-state cases. I contacted several Florida attorneys. Many would not take an out-of-state client, and the ones who would take the case wanted a huge retainer. They said the case wasn't strong enough to win and that by the time it went to trial, if it ever did, my father would most likely be dead.

I was facing a difficult decision. I could quit law school, leave my family, and move to Florida. Another thought ran across my mind. With a phone call to my friend Debbie Biggica, a lovely Italian lady who lived in Orlando and had "connections," I could remove Gail from all our lives—permanently. However, since it would have been difficult for me to take the bar exam with a felony conviction, I had to find another solution to the problem.

I ran an Internet search for senior financial abuse in the state of Florida. I discovered Florida.com. I found exactly what I was looking for on their web page: "Reporting Abuse/Neglect/Exploitation" and an 800 number for the Florida Abuse Hotline. On Sunday, July 4, 2004, I placed the call that began my very own Independence Day Revolution.

Chapter 5

Eleanor Parker, protective investigator from the Florida Department of Children and Families, returned my phone call at 9:30 Monday morning, July 5, 2004. We spoke at length regarding my cousin's actions. She said she would visit my father in the nursing home, interview Gail, and get back to me as soon as she had the information needed to proceed with the next step. In the meantime, she suggested I contact the police and file a report under Florida Statute 825.103: Exploitation of an elderly person or disabled adult.

Under Florida statute, the legal definition of "Exploitation of an elderly person or disabled adult" means:

(a) Knowingly, by deception or intimidation, obtaining or using, or endeavoring to obtain or use, an elderly person's or disabled adult's funds, assets, or property with the intent to temporarily or permanently deprive the elderly person or disabled adult of the use, benefit, or possession of the funds, assets, or property, or to benefit someone other than the elderly person or disabled adult, by a person who: 1. Stands in a position of trust and confidence with the elderly person or disabled adult; or 2. Has a business relationship with the elderly person or disabled adult; or

(b) Obtaining or using, endeavoring to obtain or use, or conspiring with another to obtain or use an elderly person's or disabled adult's funds, assets, or property with the intent to temporarily or permanently deprive the elderly person or disabled adult of the use, benefit, or possession of the funds, assets, or property, or to benefit someone other than the elderly person or disabled adult, by a person who knows or reasonably should know that the elderly person or disabled adult lacks the capacity to consent.

When I read this, I was thrilled! According to the statute, Gail had broken the law. My next call was to report her to the Florida police.

The Palm Beach police detective immediately filed the report, arrested Gail, and threw her in jail for the rest of her life. Nice scenarios, if this were an episode of *Law and Order*. However, in reality, Detective Keith Conley interviewed Gail and visited the nursing home to speak with my father. A few days later, he reported to me that although Dad was a very nice guy, there wasn't anything further he could do on the case. Gail had told him I had brought my parents' income tax refund check to Florida, and that I could be accused of impropriety. I tried to explain to the detective that half the amount of the check had been sent to my father's attorney, the other half was with my mother's attorney, and there were no grounds at all for any suspicious activities. He refused to believe me.

When I told Eleanor what had happened, she was furious. If the police were unwilling to stop her, Gail would retain control over my father and his assets unless we could find another solution. Eleanor suggested that she could file a petition and request a Temporary Emergency Guardian for my father, and the court would appoint an agency to temporarily control Dad's finances, end the divorce, protect him from Gail, and return him to Ellenville. She suggested Jewish Family Services because I lived out of state and was ineligible to be appointed guardian. (A fact I discovered much later to be false). I was greatly relieved. Our family is Jewish. The organization is Jewish. What better group to help us than Jewish Family Services?

Before agreeing to this, I phoned Jewish Family Services and spoke with Lee Eakin, the head of their guardianship program. I explained, in detail, the "emergency" regarding my cousin Gail, and he agreed that a Temporary Emergency Guardianship was exactly the remedy I was searching for. Lee explained to me that once my father was declared incapacitated, Jewish Family Services would assume guardianship for sixty days, which would give us plenty of time to make the necessary arrangements to return my father to New York. Lee told me he'd handled cases like this before and there would only be a nominal fee for their services. He seemed so supportive and understanding, especially when he told me "not to worry."

This solution sounded so perfect I couldn't believe it!

Five days after I made the call to the Florida hot line, Eleanor filed the petition with the court. Everything was agreed to and legally filed with the courts. On July 9, 2004, my cousin's power of attorney and all access to our family's finances was ended.

Finally, I had the help I'd been searching for! At that point, it was my belief that within one month, Dad would be back with our family and my life could return to normal.

On July 26, I faxed Lee a list of specific actions our family wished for him to address during the sixty-day emergency guardianship appointment. Lee read through the letter, and agreed to each of my requests.

Since much of the petition for the Temporary Emergency Guardianship involved Gail, Lee said he would contact the administrator of Boulevard Manor Nursing Home, Steve, and their social services administrator, Maureen, to inform them that Gail and her "friend" Sylvia Gardner were prohibited from any contact with my father while he was a patient at the nursing home. To prevent Gail from withdrawing any more money, Lee said he would close all accounts jointly held by Gail and my father and change the beneficiary on Dad's IRA accounts back to my daughters.

I also asked Lee to inform the medical personnel that any information regarding treatment, medications, and medical procedures including surgery, dialysis, angiogram, or any other change in Dad's physical or mental state must be reported to my mother or myself and that we were to be listed as next of kin on all medical forms. I also requested the he have Dad's medical records transferred to Dr. Walter Sperling, Dad's primary physician in Ellenville, so that we could arrange to have Dad cared for after he returned home. Lee assured me there would be no problem and that I shouldn't worry. He also agreed with me that due to Dad's dementia, Lee would personally contact Attorney Raab and have the divorce action dismissed.

Lee politely asked if I would send a complete financial statement of accounts held in my father's name so that he could see what moneys Gail had depleted and how much money Howard Raab had been paid. He said that he wanted to make sure no one else had any access to Dad's funds. At the time, Lee seemed so helpful that his request sounded reasonable. I had no reason to suspect that he had ulterior motives for requesting the financial information. I foolishly gave him the complete list of banks, insurance holdings, and investment account numbers and amounts that were in my dad's name.

With everything agreed to, and only two months before my father could come home, I felt our nightmare would soon be over.

Little did I realize it was only just beginning.

On the telephone, Lee had been pleasant and empathetic. He had agreed to address all of our concerns with my dad. He even stated that, according to Florida law, the Temporary Emergency Guardian's first and most important job was to find a qualified relative to assume the responsibility over their ward. What was even more exciting was that, under Florida law, daughters received priority even over cousins!

Lee was very supportive and confident in telling me that Dad would be returned to our family in a few weeks and that Gail would no longer be a threat. I should have become suspicious when I mentioned to him that I was thinking about attending the September court hearing in Florida. Even though it was the first week of law school, I felt that I needed to be there in order to pick up my Dad. Lee's kind voice immediately changed to a slightly irritated tone. He said it wasn't necessary for me to come to Florida because once the Temporary Emergency Guardianship was ordered terminated, he would see to it that Dad was sent home. He continued to assure me that my father was being well taken care of and that I had nothing to worry about.

I phoned my mother and gave her all the information. I was confident that everything was going to be all right since Gail was no longer a threat to Mom's financial security and I trusted Lee. After all, Lee was from a JEWISH organization and had been totally up front with me about everything his agency was going to do to help our family.

Back in Florida, it was a totally different story. No one at the Florida Department of Children and Family Services or Jewish Family Services, a *non-profit agency*, had ever mentioned that the guardian received a *substantial* fee—in the thousands—for their services, and that the fee was paid from the assets of their ward. No one had mentioned that the guardian also hired expensive law firms who charged for reading and writing letters, sending and receiving faxes, making and receiving telephone calls, eating, drinking, pissing (ok, that's a bit of a stretch), all sanctioned by the probate courts as "reasonable fees" and paid from the estate of the ward!

My evil cousin, the financial vampire, had been replaced with even more vicious blood-sucking demons: Jewish Family Services and the law firm of Shalloway and Shalloway. Publicly, G. Mark Shalloway was a strong advocate for seniors in Florida. His professional credentials were numerous, including serving as the vice president of the National Academy of Elder Law Attorneys. Before the ink had time to dry on the court order giving Temporary Emergency Guardianship to the Jewish Family Services, this public "advocate" against senior financial abuse privately began charging attorney fees at a rate of $275 an hour. Once my father's life savings fell into the hands of Jewish Family Services, they had carte blanche to pay whatever fees they desired from our family's estate, with full approval of the Florida probate court.

Jewish Family Services and the law firm of Shalloway and Shalloway were now draining every dime my parents had worked their entire lives to save. In effect, they had hooked a hose to my parents' financial security and on July 14, 2004, a scant five days after Eleanor Parker filed the Temporary Emergency Guardianship petition to protect my father from financial exploitation and abuse, Lee Eakin and Mark Shalloway switched on the "vacuum"—and it really sucked.

Chapter 6

The summer passed quickly. With Gail's influence over Dad's communications out of the picture, I was able to talk to him on a regular basis. Even though Dad didn't have a phone in his room, the nurses were nice enough to let him use their cell phones and everyone formed a very nice long distance relationship. Because of this, I was also able to obtain information on his health and mental condition, which seemed to be improving. He constantly inquired about Mom and his grandchildren, saying how much he missed them, and that he was looking forward to coming to California when he was feeling better.

Dad sounded so optimistic that it was difficult to remember he was in a nursing home and in need of constant medical attention.

I began to make plans to find a rehabilitation facility near Ellenville. I sent an email to my high school friend, Elliot Auerbach, who was now the Ellenville Village Manager. His mother was in a nursing home due to Alzheimer. Elliot sent me information on several facilities near Ellenville that would have been suitable for Dad, but they all needed specific medical information from his Florida facility before they would be able to admit him. I phoned Steve Mellison, the administrator at Boulevard Manor, who said faxing the information wouldn't be a problem once Dad no longer had Jewish Family Services as his guardian.

I phoned Lee with the news that I had made arrangements for Dad's care after he returned home and that I looked forward to meeting him in person at the hearing. Lee mentioned that Dad would also be at the hearing. He explained that at the hearing procedure, the judge would first rule on Dad's capacity before deciding to release Jewish Family Services as the guardian. He assured me this wouldn't be a problem since Dad was going to be at the hearing and was doing so well that he didn't need a guardian. I asked Lee if he thought I needed my own attorney, and he stated I didn't because the court had appointed an attorney for Dad, so he would have adequate representation at the hearing. He restated his assertion that I couldn't petition for guardianship because I did not live in Florida; but, in this case, it wouldn't be necessary.

The first week of September was also the first week of law school. It was also the middle of Florida's hurricane season. However, neither rain, sleet, school, nor the threat of a Florida hurricane was going to keep me from attending the hearing.

Vic met my plane and drove me to the hotel, which was only a few blocks from the courthouse. It was nice to see a friendly face! I told him about the hearing and that I was confident by this time the next day, my Dad would be on his way home. Vic said he hoped I was right; but after living in South Florida for over twenty years, he was a bit skeptical. He had read about situations where families had lost thousands of dollars fighting against a guardianship. He was also concerned about the weather. There were numerous warnings being posted for Hurricane Frances, and he needed to stock up on emergency supplies and board up his windows, so he wouldn't be able to attend the hearing with me.

To help take my mind off the situation I was facing, Vic and I went to dinner and talked about my daughters, and old friends from high school. I told him how much I hated

Florida and joked that California has its own seasons: fire, flood, drought, and earthquakes, which hit without any warnings from the National Weather Bureau but that we also had mountains and zero humidity. Like a hurricane, our evening together was the calm before the storm; but like an earthquake, I never received any warning about the devastation that was to come.

Early Wednesday morning, I called a taxi and arrived at the courthouse at 8:30 for the 9:00 hearing. After going through security, I found the room where the hearing was going to be held. The waiting area outside the courtroom was empty when I arrived. I was anxious to meet Eleanor and Lee, whom I had only spoken to on the phone. I was even more anxious to see Dad to assure him that we'd have him home by the end of the day.

As I read through my notes, an elderly man sat down across from me. I introduced myself as Raven West, my California pen name, as I didn't wish to reveal my true identity to anyone I didn't know. Not knowing my real name, this man started speaking about my father, and how very sad it was that he was caught up in such a nasty fight with his daughter. I started to get nervous. The man turned out to be Stanley Rosenstock, a friend of my father, but I still felt it best not to reveal my identity. This ruse lasted about three seconds when another man came into the waiting room and sat next to Stanley. He looked at me and said, "Hello, Robin." I didn't recognize him though, so I responded with a "hi" and waited to see what would happen next. When the man left, I asked Stanley who he was. To my horror, Stanley said he was Gail's brother Robert, my other cousin who I'd not seen or spoken to in over thirty-five years. I had no idea why he or Stanley was attending my father's capacity hearing.

Several minutes later, a woman walked in and introduced herself to me as Eleanor Parker. She pointed to a large gentleman and said he was Lee Eakin from Jewish Family Services. I walked over to Lee. He was talking on his cell phone so I waited for him to complete the call, and then introduced myself. For some reason, I felt that Lee was reluctant to talk with me. I asked him why Stanley and Gail's brother and his wife were at the hearing, and if he thought they were up to something. Lee had no idea why they were there or why they were in a huddled conversation with Howard Raab.

What was a divorce attorney doing in probate court talking to Gail's brother? I was afraid to speculate. I could only surmise that he was going to file for guardianship and that the divorce attorney was now representing Robert.

There was a knot forming in my stomach. I had to remind myself that I was in law school and had better be able to handle myself in a professional manner in a courtroom, even if my emotional state was quickly rising to the level of attack mode.

Court was called to order a few minutes past nine. It was standing room only inside the small courtroom. My cousin and his wife; Stanley Rosenstock; Eleanor Parker and her associate; a few doctors; Dad's court-appointed attorney, David Centola; Lee Eakin from Jewish Family Services; their attorney, Mark Shalloway; and Howard Raab were all in attendance. It seemed to me as if everyone in the state of Florida was crowded into that courtroom except the one person who was, by Florida statute, supposed to be there—my father.

The Florida court was a totally different experience than the courts in California. California courts record all their hearings with a court reporter, but there was none present in this Florida courtroom. When the bailiff announced the judge's entrance, Judge Gary Vonhof entered wearing a casual business suit. He told everyone to remain seated. However, once the proceedings began, it was all business— and all the business was nothing that I had expected.

Judge Vonhof looked first through the medical reports regarding my father's capacity. He asked one of the doctors if Dad was completely incapacitated, according to the medical examiner's reports, which I had never seen. I knew my dad had been diagnosed with mild dementia from the medical reports I had obtained in May, but anyone who met him could tell he was in no way "completely" out of it. Had my father been in the courtroom, the judge could have seen for himself, and not had to rely only on a medical report and some doctor's ten-minute examination. Without any way for Dad to defend himself, and with the confirmation of the doctor's assessment of his incapacity, the judge made his ruling and in instantly all of my father's constitutionally protected fundamental rights were taken away from him, including his right to decide where he wanted to live.

When it came time to determine the question of guardianship, Judge Vonhof questioned Eleanor Parker about the call made to the Florida senior abuse hot line, but she never mentioned that I was the one who had made the call or the reason for the Temporary Emergency Guardianship petition.

Then, Howard Raab gave testimony against my mother, mentioning that she had not appeared for a deposition in New York. In my opinion, this had nothing to do with the case and I sent very strong visual stares at what Raab because of what he was saying, but this only resulted in my getting a reprimand from the judge. Raab conveniently failed to mention that the reason my mother didn't attend the deposition was because she was in the hospital at the time. I was trying without much success to maintain my composure, but when Stanley gave his testimony that Dad was happy and wanted to stay in Florida, followed by my cousin's similar lies, I nearly lost it.

Then it was my turn to speak. I first apologized to the judge for my behavior regarding Raab. I said I was Ruby Cohen's daughter from California and had flown to Florida to take him home to New York. On very wobbly legs, I had to stand up in a court of law in front of strangers and defend my love for my own father. I clarified that I was the one who had called the hot line and the reasons why. I testified that, contrary to what other people had said, my father wanted to go home to New York and to visit his family in California. I was nearly in tears and completely lost the professionalism I had hoped to maintain during the proceedings.

Judge Vonhof listened to my testimony, said thank you, and asked me to sit down, which I did. I held my breath while he determined the fate of my father. Judge Vonhof began looking through his papers, and then made a comment that he didn't see any other petitions for guardianship. At that moment, I expected Lee Eakin to step up and request that the guardianship be transferred to me. I waited, and waited, but he just sat silently in his chair, avoiding looking in my direction. I noticed my cousin and Raab whispering to each other in the back of the room, and I started to panic. What other reason could they possibly have had for attending the hearing if not to file their own petition for guardianship?

I was terrified Raab was going to pull a guardianship petition out of his briefcase and, without any support in opposition, I felt completely helpless to prevent this from happening. I didn't have an attorney because I had been told I didn't need one. I hadn't filed a guardianship petition because I had been told, since I lived out of state, I couldn't. Now it appeared there was no legal way I could prevent my cousins from getting full, legal, and permanent control over my father and our family's estate if they so chose.

After everything I'd been through to get Gail removed from our lives, short of hiring a hit man, I wasn't about to let her or her brother score a legal victory. When Judge Vonhof asked me if I had any objections to Jewish Family Services becoming Dad's permanent guardian, I felt totally backed into a corner. Had I not agreed, I felt certain my cousin Robert would start the proceeding to have himself declared Dad's guardian.

I'd been lied to by Lee Eakin; blind-sided by Howard Raab and my cousins, Gail and Robert; let down by Eleanor Parker; and bulldozed by a very well-oiled Florida guardianship machine comprised of the Jewish Family Services, a team of psychologists, attorneys, and a Florida probate judge. It was either agree to allow Jewish Family Services to assume permanent "temporary" guardianship, or watch my cousins use the legal system to help them take my father away from my family and me.

In any war, one must lose a few small battles in order to win the final victory. In an uncharacteristically meek voice I responded, "I guess so."

With a bang of his gavel, Judge Vonhof set the wheels in motion for what would become my own personal vendetta against the forces of guardianship injustice in every state across the nation.

Chapter 7

I walked out of the courtroom in a daze. After expecting to be able to take my father home, I was left with no idea how I was going to accomplish this now that Jewish Family Services had secured a permanent guardianship status over my father's life.

Eleanor Parker met me outside the courthouse and offered to drive me to the nursing home where Dad was staying. On the way, I asked her what I should do next. She had no idea. She explained that once the Florida Department of Children and Family Services handed the case over to the courts, her job was finished. Eleanor dropped me off at Boulevard Manor, wished me luck, and drove off. I ran inside the facility and immediately spotted Dad talking to my cousin Robert and his wife, who left the instant they saw me. Dad was wearing an ugly Florida print shirt, mismatched pants, and his hair was in an unflattering buzz cut. In spite of his outward appearance, his bright blue eyes still had the same sparkle, one of the physical traits handed down from father to daughter, to his grandchildren.

We talked a few minutes about his health, and why I had come to Florida. I told him about the court appearance and asked him why he hadn't been there. Dad said he had been told he was going to the hearing, and that he had been waiting for someone to pick him up but no one ever came for him. He wanted me to stay a few days, but I explained I had to leave that afternoon because a hurricane was on the way and they were threatening to close the airports. He was sad that I had to leave, but said he understood.

We ate lunch together in the facility. When we went into the dining room, a woman named "Cookie" sat down and started to help him eat. Dad seemed to know her, and I thought she was a staff member at the facility. Cookie put milk and sweetener in Dad's coffee cup, which was strange because Dad always drank his coffee black and liked it in a glass. I asked Dad when he had started drinking coffee that way, and he said he always did. A chill ran up my spine. Although he looked a bit frail, Dad appeared to be getting back to normal. It wasn't until I had a chance to talk with him alone that I realized his road back to "normal" had taken a serious detour.

After Cookie left, Dad and I finally had a chance to talk alone. Dad said he was very unhappy being in the "hotel." He asked me when I was going to get him "out of here" and said how much he wanted to come to California to see his grandchildren. I asked him if he had received the photos of our family I had sent to him and a picture that Tandy had painted for his room, but said he didn't remember receiving them. When I brought him back to his room after lunch, I found the mail I had sent to him, along with the pictures, stuffed into a drawer, while pictures of Gail and my other cousins were hanging on the wall. He also told me he had never received the letters I had sent him. I thought his mental condition might have affected his memory, but he recalled the letters from my daughters, the ones that Cookie had read to him.

I still had no idea who Cookie was, or why she was so involved with my father. She had left after lunch before I had a chance to ask her. Dad decided to take a nap so I told him I'd be back early in the morning before he left for dialysis.

On my way out, I asked the nurse at the front desk to show me the medical list, to see if there was a person named "Cookie" on it. Much to my dismay, Gail's name was listed as emergency contact, right beneath Lee Eakin's as guardian. No other names were listed. After meeting with the social services director, Maureen, I added the rest of our family to the next of kin list. Once they met me in person, it was easier to obtain the information I needed. Maureen told me Dad was on dialysis three times a week, his blood sugar was still unstable, and that he would probably be in the nursing home for another month or more. I told her that it was imperative I be contacted should my father be moved to another facility, because my cousin had moved him in the past without any of us knowing where he was. She assured me that Gail no longer had the authority to take that kind of action now that Jewish Family Services was Dad's legal guardian, and that she would definitely call me if Dad were moved.

I took a taxi out to the offices of JFS, at a cost of $45, to meet with Lee about what was going to happen to my dad. Because of the imminent hurricane, most of the staff had already left, including Lee, so I met with Neil Newstein, Jewish Family Services executive director. I asked Neil about the divorce. Now that Dad had been declared incapacitated, he couldn't sue or be sued, and I wanted the proceedings ended immediately. Neil said they were going to "look into it." I mentioned Gail's involvement and how were we going to protect our family's assets if Dad had a guardian. Neil said not to worry; JFS would only use funds to take care of Dad's medical needs and would pay themselves a small fee of about $140 a month for their services. I asked how soon they would proceed with my requests of changing the beneficiaries from my cousins back to my children and ending the divorce proceedings, but Neil avoided my questions and had to call the meeting short because of the weather. However, he assured me he would contact me as soon as he could.

I had no other choice but to call another taxi, spend an additional $45, and return to my hotel. The following morning, I went back to see my father before he was transported to the dialysis facility. He was still asleep when I arrived, so I sat in the chair and waited for him to wake up. He was so glad I was there. We had breakfast, thankfully alone, and had a chance to talk about his heath. I asked him if he knew what had happened since I'd seen him in the hospital last May.

To my shock and dismay, Dad didn't remember my visit. He didn't even remember being in the hospital, or undergoing a by-pass surgery to improve the circulation in his leg to fix the ulcer in his heel. I didn't want him to see how hard it was for me to keep the tears from forming. I desperately wanted to grab my father, throw him into my car and head for the airport but with his poor health, need for dialysis treatments, and with Jewish Family Services now pulling all the legal strings, I was helpless to take any action at all.

When the transport arrived, I accompanied Dad to the van. I was nearly hysterical when he looked at me and said, "I'm sorry." I told him it wasn't his fault, and no matter what anyone said or wrote in a medical record, I would always be his daughter. We hugged, kissed, and I cried as the transport drove my father away that early September morning. I felt this would be the very last time I ever saw my father. The gray clouds forming overhead mirrored the devastating sense of loss that was forming over my soul.

I left Florida on the last plane out of Ft. Lauderdale before they closed the airport. Over the next few days, I tried to call the Jewish Family Services but their office had closed due to the hurricane. The switchboard at the Boulevard Manor was only taking emergency phone calls. The phone lines were down all over that area of Florida for nearly a week after the hurricane. I was frantic with worry about my father's health. Because of the three-hour time difference, I had to wake up at six in the morning in order to reach Florida and to call New York to check on my mother, whose heath was rapidly deteriorating.

Since my father didn't have a telephone in his room, there was no way he could contact me and it was several days later before I was able to talk to him. Thankfully, the facility had made it through the worst of the storm, and Dad had been able to go to his dialysis treatments without any delays. He sounded fine, but we could never talk very long since we were using the nurse's cell phone. The situation was difficult, but at least Dad was safe and his medical needs were being met.

I continued calling Jewish Family Services and leaving messages. The offices were closed for the Jewish High Holy Days of Rosh Hashanah and Yom Kippur, so no one answered my calls. I phoned my dad's accountant to find out if the names on the beneficiary had been changed as Lee and I had agreed he would do, and I contacted Mom's New York attorney regarding dismissing the divorce. Neither my mother nor her attorney had received any notice of a dismissal. Instead, there were more bills for phone calls and faxes to the divorce attorney, and the law offices of Shalloway and Shalloway were now charging for their fees whenever they contacted Howard Raab. In effect, the attorneys would meet in the bathroom: one took a piss, the other wiped it off, and they *both* charged my father for the privilege!

As soon as their offices reopened, Jewish Family Services wasted no time in going through every financial piece of information that I had unwittingly supplied to Lee. My father's New York accountant phoned and informed me that his office had received a letter from Dad's "guardian" instructing them to close out all of my father's accounts and send the money to them. He said legally there wasn't anything they could do about it except to comply. Between the two accounts, Jewish Family Services had depleted over $125,000; and what was even more disturbing; they had specifically requested that none of the moneys be held for taxes.

My parents were still legally married, and even though the IRAs were in my father's name alone, both of them owned the property. Any income derived from the liquidation of the annuities would be taxable income, and any taxes owed or penalties for early withdrawal would come from both my parents, even though my mother received no income at all from the IRAs.

In less than one month after receiving their permanent guardianship appointment, Jewish Family Services had liquidated all of my father's retirement annuities, half of the mortgage payments on the sale of the bakery, and had cashed in my father's social security checks. Every dime that had been in my father's checking and savings accounts had been transferred into the guardianship account of Jewish Family Services, and they now had carte blanche to use these funds to pay all of their expenses, including huge attorney fees to Howard Raab and G. Mark Shalloway.

What was even more infuriating was that in spite of all the assurances I had received from Jewish Family Services, the Florida Department of Children and Family

Services, and the staff at Boulevard Manor Nursing Home, my cousin Gail continued to have full access to my father. She was even paid over $2,000 from my father's account. Although the reason for the "emergency" that Eleanor Parker had petitioned the court to remedy was to prevent Gail from obtaining money from my father, she continued doing so with the court's approval!

From the first call to the Florida hot line, everything I had been told had been a lie. The original court order, regarding the reason for Temporary Emergency Guardianship, had been ignored. What I'd been told regarding my inability to petition for guardianship wasn't true. Unless I could find the time and money to travel back and forth to Florida, I was facing the possibility of never seeing my father again. What was even more heartbreaking was the possibility that my children would most likely never see their grandfather, and that my mother would be left with no financial support to survive another freezing New York winter.

All this tragedy occurred as a direct result of my cousin Gail's actions, and my other cousins' refusal to help me stop her before it was too late.

It was way past being too late.

Chapter 8

By October 2004, my father was virtually a prisoner in the state of Florida. My mother was all alone in a small town in upstate New York while a well-oiled guardianship machine in another state was rapidly depleting the money she needed for living expenses, including heat, electricity, property taxes, and mounting attorney fees. Mom had become depressed to the point where she stopped eating. As a result, her weight had dropped to eighty pounds and she was getting weaker by the day.

I called Mom several times a week, and on many occasions she told me that Vickie, the hospital nurse, was visiting and taking care of her. Mom said she was doing fine, but her stories of people coming into the house, or hiding things, began to concern me. My parents had installed a security system years ago so I phoned the company. They told me there had been no security breaches at that address, although Mom insisted someone had been in the house.

Even though Mom had a neighbor install chain locks on all the doors, they failed to keep out the stray cats that were now running wild inside the house. My mother owned a very large dog that was now a danger because he was running all over the house chasing the cats. I was receiving reports from Vickie that the house was starting to smell from the stench of animal excrement, there were newspapers and garbage everywhere, and that she was becoming increasingly concerned about the decline of my mother's mental and physical condition.

A week before Halloween, I phoned Mom and Vickie answered. She told me that my mother was in the hospital after having fallen in the house the previous night. Somehow, Mom had managed to crawl to the phone and dial the Ellenville First Aid Squad, which had taken her to the emergency room. I phoned the hospital and spoke to my mother. Fortunately, she had only suffered a minor cut on her arm, but she was going to be in the hospital a few days for observation.

In spite of the situation with the guardianship in Florida, I knew that at least my father's health needs were being taken care of. My mother now became my primary concern. I could only deal with one parent at a time, and I couldn't deal with either one from three thousand miles away in a different time zone. "Superheroes" seldom think about consequences when they are called into action to aid someone in need, and my mother needed me. There wasn't any question as to what I had to do now.

Our family was firmly implanted in California. Michelle was starting college in Santa Barbara, Kimberly was in her second year of college in UC Davis, my husband had just started a new job, and I was in my second year of law school. In 1976 I moved to California to escape the cold winter weather, and there was no way I was moving back East. At that instant, I didn't think. I just knew what needed to be done, and I acted. Having no real plan in mind at the time, I made the only choice available—one that would change all of our lives forever.

I took a very long, deep breath, and said, "Mom, I'm flying out to New York and bringing you to California."

I waited for an argument, but I was not about to listen to any of her excuses. I knew I had to be firm because that was the only way to convince Mom that her very life depended on leaving the only home she had ever known.

Mom had lived in Ellenville her entire life. She was involved with several senior organizations. She had been honored with a "Reginia Cohen Day" a few months ago. However, many of her friends were retiring and moving to Florida, and the ones who stayed had their own families to care for. With the winter weather approaching, driving on ice-and-snow-covered roads would make it difficult, if not impossible, for emergency vehicles to reach her in case of another accident.

I had neither the time nor the energy to go into a lengthy debate. In my sternest "mom" voice that I'd perfected over the years on my three daughters, I added, "This is *not* open to discussion."

To make the idea more palatable, I told Mom that she would come to California for the winter, and then return to New York when the weather was warmer, the way her "snowbird" friends flew to and from Florida I lied.

Sometimes doing the right thing is the hardest thing to do, especially when other people lives would be affected by that "right" decision.

Our two grown daughters were away at college, and my husband and I were enjoying our "empty nest." With Mom's medical needs to consider, it would have been impossible for her to live in our home.

I called my good friend Jeffrey Greene, who had been researching adult facilities in our local area. He told me of Sunrise Assisted Living, which was only about ten miles from my house. I immediately phoned to inquire when they were going to open. As if by some divine intervention, they had just opened the day I called. I set up an appointment, took a tour of their brand new facility, and signed the papers that day. Sunrise had 24-hour medical care, a wonderful staff, and excellent food. The room I picked for Mom was a two-room apartment with a beautiful view of the mountains, similar to those of the Catskills, so she wouldn't be too homesick. I arranged for a moving company to meet us in New York to transport some of my mother's furniture so she would have her own bed and feel at "home" in her new environment.

On Halloween Eve, 2004, this "not-so-wicked Witch of the West" hopped on her broomstick and headed east.

The devastation as a result of my cousin's interference in my family's lives was apparent the moment I walked into what had been our home for over forty years. When my mother opened the door, she was completely doubled over. At first, I thought she was looking for something on the floor, but she had been "looking" since the middle of October. Mom was so weak that she had to raise her chin off her chest with one hand and eat through a straw. I couldn't believe her nurse had never told me how sick she'd become, or that my mother had never mentioned anything to me. With the stress of the impending divorce, my father's inability to communicate with her, and facing the potential loss of her home, it was as if she'd simply given up on life. I'd arrived "in the nick of time."

I went on autopilot. Within one week's time, I packed up her belongings, closed down the utilities in the house, closed out the bank accounts, and put Mom on a plane to California—first class.

I also fired her divorce attorney.

Mom stayed in my house until her furniture arrived. She moved into her new home three days prior to her birthday. On November 16, 2004, my husband, our three daughters, and I celebrated my mother's very happy birthday together. The one person who was missing from this otherwise perfect family portrait was my father.

Chapter 9

December has always been a very special month for our family. Dad's birthday is on the sixth, my daughter Michelle's is on the seventh, and mine is the eleventh. When the children were younger, we would also celebrate all eight nights of Hanukkah, with plenty of presents and latkes, singing and dancing for almost the entire month. My parents would visit annually to celebrate our very special holiday of "Hanubirthday" which lasted straight on to New Year's Eve. These were some of the cherished, loving times I knew we would never enjoy again as long as my father remained in Florida. Although we had many photographs and videos of family birthdays, Bat Mitzvahs, and other holiday memories to enjoy, my father had none of these in his desolate room at the Boulevard Manor Nursing Home. With his failing memory, I was also very concerned that he would not remember any of these family occasions, or, worse, that Gail would do her best to make him forget his family altogether.

On December 6, 2004, I phoned Dad to wish him a happy birthday. He was very excited to hear from me and to let me know that he was moving out of the nursing home. I asked him where he was moving but he said he didn't know. My blood froze. In spite of Lee's commitment to inform me of my father's location, someone was moving him again. We had no idea who or why or where. It seemed as if the nightmare was starting all over again. Fortunately, I had maintained an excellent relationship with Maureen at Boulevard Manor. She told me Dad's health had improved and that he was being transferred to the Sunrise Assisted Living in Boynton Beach.

At least that was good news, but I was furious that Lee hadn't told me Dad was moving. I phoned the offices of Jewish Family Services and left a message on Lee's answering machine. Then I called the Sunrise facility to make sure they knew to contact me if there were any problems. The receptionist was less than cordial, saying only that she couldn't give out any information unless the legal guardian gave his permission. According to their records, the only contacts on their emergency contact list were Jewish Family Services and Gail Lerner.

This was the worst possible news I could have heard. After everything we had gone through to get my cousin out of the way, not only was she still in my father's life, but, apparently, our family had been erased from all of Dad's official records. There was not one entry stating he had any "next of kin" other than a niece!

When I was finally able to talk to Lee, he apologized for not telling me that Dad was being moved. He promised that he'd make sure the staff at Sunrise knew I was his daughter and to give me total access to my father.

I phoned Sunrise a few days later to see how Dad was and to talk to him. I was told he had gone out with someone. I asked who he went out with, where did he go, and when would he be back. The receptionist could only tell me that someone named "Cookie" had been coming around once a week and would take Dad out of the facility. She couldn't tell me who Cookie was or where they went, but said I should contact the guardian if I wanted more information.

I was livid. When I'd met Cookie, I was under the impression she worked for the Boulevard Manor Nursing Home. I didn't know why Cookie was allowed access to my father, or where she was taking him, and no one would tell me unless I got permission from a stranger!

I had to talk to my father.

Again, I phoned Lee and requested that he order phone service to be installed in Dad's room, and asked him who Cookie was and why she was taking Dad out of the facility. Lee said he would look into it and would order a phone installed in Dad's room. In the meantime, he said he was sending me a copy of Howard Raab's court petition to pay attorney fees for the divorce. Again, Lee assured me that Jewish Family Services was going to contest the fees and seek to discontinue the actions petitioned. Then he added, "Don't worry."

In spite of what he had told me, I was becoming increasingly suspicious of Lee's promises. Days passed and Dad still did not have phone service. The staff at the Sunrise facility was becoming increasingly belligerent when I would call and try to speak to my father. When the phone service was finally connected, I discovered that Lee had put a block on Dad's phone so that he could not make any long distance phone calls. It was obvious that Lee didn't want my father to have access to his family. However, he didn't count on the fact that it only took one phone call from me to the Florida phone company to have the block removed.

Once our family was able to communicate with Dad, we discovered a great deal more disturbing news.

Dad asked me how my mother was doing and said he was looking forward to coming to California for his birthday and seeing his grandchildren. I had to remind him his birthday had already passed. I asked him if he had told anyone about dismissing the divorce proceedings. I knew we were in serious trouble when he answered, "Did your mother file for divorce?"

"No, Dad. You did," I reminded him.

"You're crazy, I never did that."

I knew it was senseless to argue with him, so I changed the subject.

"Dad, who is Cookie?"

I could hear a chuckle in his voice when he replied, "She's my girlfriend."

After that conversation, I knew Dad's mental faculties were far from normal. With Gail having continued access, Dad would believe anything she told him. The guardian had done little to address the seriousness of the problem and, in fact, had made the situation ten times worse than it had been. Unless I could get my father away from my cousin's influence and reunite him with our family, I was convinced we would lose him forever.

This "action hero," all by myself, had successfully rescued one parent from near-death. Now it was time for me to focus my abilities to get my father out of Florida. For this, I needed the help of a more common advocate for justice: an attorney.

Attending law school had now become an asset that I had never expected, but one that I was very grateful to have. As a law student, I was required to register with the California Bar Association, but for the foundation of a legal profession, I had also become a member of the local Ventura County Bar Association.

On the recommendation of several members, I contacted an elder law attorney, Loye M. Barton. Our first meeting seemed very hopeful, but once we began discussing the process to file for a transfer of guardianship, (conservatorship in California), I became pessimistic after I learned I first had to relocate my father from Florida to California and that attorney fees, posting a bond, and a court hearing could run into thousand of dollars. The fact the current guardian was in a different state also made the situation more complicated. With the court system as full as it was, a conservatorship could take a very long time.

My father was close to eighty-four years old and in precarious health. With the Florida guardian having unlimited access to our family's assets, time and money were two luxuries neither my father nor I possessed. Gail's initial slash into my father's bank accounts had begun the bleeding of our family's finances. With Jewish Family Services and their attorneys wielding the blade, the wound had become a financial hemorrhage.

I began a furious letter-writing campaign. I sent letters to every newspaper and television station in Florida, but soon found out that this type of news was business as usual in the Sunshine State. I then began a very frustrating search for an agency or government-elected official anywhere in the state of Florida or in Washington, D.C. who could help us.

I sent a letter to Lois J. Frankel, the mayor of the city of West Palm Beach. I had read her biography on her web site and was encouraged to read that she had not only been elected as mayor of West Palm Beach, but had also served in the Florida House of Representatives for fourteen years as an energetic champion of Florida's seniors. Since she also was a member of the board of trustees of Jewish Family Services, I was certain she would use her political influence to help our family. My letter went unanswered but I received a phone call from her assistant informing me there wasn't anything Mayor Frankel could do.

I received a response from Florida State Attorney General Charlie Crist's office, with a nice letter of empathy and a list of agencies he would refer my letters to, including the head of the Department of Children and Family Services, the agency who instigated the guardianship mess in the first place.

It was an insane game of Monopoly, always going back to "start" while my father's piece sat on the corner "jail" square, and all the other players were selling off and spending all of his assets.

Letters to every elected official, from Tom Gallagher of the Florida Department of Financial Services; to Mel Martinez, Florida's United States Senator; and even to Governor Bush and the FBI, solicited a similar response. The case was out of their jurisdiction; there was nothing they could do; it was a civil matter; and they suggested I hire a good attorney.

With the guardian agency using my father's money to pay their attorneys to fight the case, no one offered any advice as to where I was going to find the funds to pay an attorney to fight against them.

It was a lose-lose situation, but it seemed I had no choice.

California attorneys cannot try cases in Florida. I needed an attorney in the jurisdiction where the probate court case was being heard; one who wouldn't demand a huge retainer; and, one who would, hopefully, have the integrity, fortitude, and empathy to take our case and help get my father home. None of the attorneys I spoke with in California had any experience with Florida guardianship cases, nor did they know anyone they could refer me to in Florida.

I was left with the only alternative: the Internet. I ran a search for elder law attorneys who met my criteria.

The first one I phoned listened to my case for about three minutes, and then quoted me a retainer of $5,000, at $350 an hour, saying, "I'm expensive because I'm worth it." She might have thought so, but true or not, we couldn't afford to pay for such a high-priced attorney, not even if she was "Denny Crane," the fictional self-important attorney on ABC-TV *Boston Legal*.

My next call was to an attorney who restored my faith in the legal profession of which I was intending to become a part: Sheri L. Hazeltine, Elder Law, Estate Planning, and Advocacy. I was especially impressed by the "Advocacy" part of her title. I phoned her office and we spoke at length. She said the case sounded fairly easy, a simple transfer of guardianship. Since I was the daughter, she said that there was no question that I was the best, and certainly the legal choice to take care of my father. Even better, she quoted a much more reasonable fee. She was warm and friendly, and exactly the type of person I was looking for to help with the legal part of the guardianship issue. I was totally confident that we would have my father with us, possibly as soon as Passover.

Sheri said she would file the papers the next day. Then she said the two little words I had come to despise: "Don't worry."

Chapter 10

One of the advantages of having access to the Internet is the ability to find documents that, in the past, would have required a great deal of time and expense. With a simple search for Florida's court records, I was able to locate the entire case description and docket information on my father's guardianship case. After reading several of the entries, I had no doubt that Lee Eakin did not intend to help our family.

Despite statements from Lee that Jewish Family Services would file to dismiss the divorce action, on August 18, 2004, they had filed a "joint motion *to confirm and authorize* representation by Howard Raab as attorney for the ward in connection with dissolution of marriage." Even E. Michael Kavanagh, the Supreme Court Justice of the State of New York, was skeptical about proceeding with the divorce action. In October 2004, he sent a letter to my mother's attorney attesting to his concerns. Nevertheless, even his opinion didn't deter Howard Raab from continuing to bill additional fees for months. It wasn't until December that Jewish Family Services filed a motion to withdraw the petition for dissolution of marriage and terminate the representation of Howard Raab as counsel, giving Raab ample time to add additional charges.

When I received a fax from Lee Eakin with the entire twelve pages of Rabb's attorney fees attached, I was nauseous. During a three-month interval, Howard Raab had continued racking up attorney fees at a rate of $300 an hour. From July 29, 2004, to November 30, 2004, he billed telephone calls to Gail Lerner, communications with a number of attorneys and correspondences with Mark Shalloway, adding up to over $11,000. Not one line item

listed any contact with Raab's client, my father. With every
call to G. Mark Shalloway, there was a duplicate charge to
my father from the law offices of Shalloway and Shalloway
for the very same phone call.

Lee Eakin and the Jewish Family Services' attorney
made a token appearance at the attorney fee hearing and
billed my father for their time, but never contested the fees.
In expectation of an opposition, Raab had hired an "expert"
witness, Robert D. Arnestein, to fly down from New York
and testify to the "reasonable" fees requested; and, then
Jewish Family Services paid the witness himself $2,475 from
my father's estate! On January 25, 2005, Howard Raab
walked into the probate courtroom of the 15th District Court
in Delray Beach, Florida; and, unopposed, walked out with
over $15,000 of my parents' life savings. Although Sheri
filed a motion for a rehearing and request to stay the order on
Raab's petition for fees, the motion was denied.

The news was devastating. Even with an attorney
now working on our case, the fact that I wasn't physically in
Florida meant there was no way to stop Jewish Family
Services from depleting our entire family's entire assets and
the worst was yet to come. In addition to the petition to
terminate Howard Raab as counsel, the Shalloway law firm
began a petition for a Medicaid plan. If granted, this would
have resulted in the guardian being able to sell my parent's
New York home, and to transfer all of my father's remaining
assets into the Jewish Family Services' trust fund, with
Jewish Family Services named as beneficiary. This "plan"
also allocated $2,500 for funeral expenses, even though both
my parents' funeral arrangements had been arranged
previously through our family's synagogue in Ellenville.

For drawing up this horrific "plan," the law offices of Shalloway and Shalloway would receive an additional $8,000. If they had succeeded, Dad would be buried in an unknown grave somewhere in Southern Florida.

I was never so scared in my entire life.

The year 2004 had begun with my parents living together in the house where I grew up. The year 2004 had begun with my father's health improving under the loving care of my mother. The year 2004 was the year my cousin's interference threatened everything and everyone in my entire family.

The year 2004 ended with the possibility that my father would be taken from me forever, and thrown into a state Medicaid home. The year 2004 ended with the possibility of leaving my mother without any financial security, and the legacy of Cohen's Bakery would be given over to a nameless, cold-hearted Florida guardian and their attorneys.

The year 2005 was going to be the beginning of my discovering just how much strength and determination I had in me. It was the year I was going to become the very epitome of "Robin" Hood fighting for justice against the evil "Sheriff of Nottingham," Mark Shalloway, and his right-hand man, Sir "Guy" Eakin.

Chapter 11

Early in February, Sheri filed several motions including an interim judicial review, and a motion for inspection of the inventory and accounting of and guardianship plans for the ward. Neither of these motions went to a hearing. The information would have been invaluable for our case, but we never were able to obtain a ruling.

Under so much stress, I felt as if my shoulders were down to my knees. My law school mid-term exams were scheduled for the first week of January, but my mind wasn't on Real Property, California Community Property, or the Federal Rules of Civil Procedure. I would have given anything to have taken just one course in Florida guardianship law, which was not on the California bar exam, but, thankfully, Sheri had taken and passed the Florida bar exam.

Although it was very difficult to take advice from someone I'd only met over the phone, I needed to trust a stranger and believe in the justice system I was studying so hard to enter. After my experience with the Florida courts, trust and belief were two things in very short supply, and I never put much stock in "blind" faith.

The Medicaid plan was set to go to hearing on February 14, and Sheri was adamant that I attend. If Jewish Family Services succeeded in establishing a Medicaid plan for my father without any opposition, the court would most likely rubber stamp Jewish Family's petition as they had every other motion the Shalloway law firm had requested.

Since moving to the Sunrise Assisted Living Facility in California, my mother's health had continued to improve. She was meeting new friends while keeping in touch with her East Coast friends through email. Sarah had sent her a note that the Ellenville reunion in Florida was scheduled for the first week of February, so it seemed the perfect time for me to plan a trip. If Dad was feeling strong enough to attend, I'd go to the reunion with him and we'd have a real family reunion of our own.

There are times when even Robin Hood needs a partner. In this case, my "Little John" was my daughter Tandy. I phoned her in Oklahoma and asked if she could meet me in Florida. The two of us could visit Dad, attend the hearing together, and show the judge a loving daughter and granddaughter who wanted to bring Dad home. I made the flight arrangements, hotel and car reservations, printed out directions off Mapquest, and headed east once again.

After checking into the hotel, I drove to the Sunrise facility in Boynton Beach where Dad was now living. Having seen the accommodations in California, I expected the same quality in the Florida location. Much to my dismay, I soon discovered that not all Sunrise facilities were created equal. I went to the reception desk and introduced myself as Ruby Cohen's daughter. The woman didn't recognize the name. She said they had a "Rubin" Cohen, but no one named Ruby. It seemed as if the guardian not only had tried to rob my father of his material possession, but his very identity as well!

I located Dad's room on the second floor. He was sleeping on a cramped day bed, which was designed for a child. There was a second-hand dresser by the wall, two very ugly chairs, a small table with a telephone, and a television set in the corner. The walls were void of any family photos, and the room smelled of disinfectant. Dad woke up and was totally thrilled to see me. He was extremely happy when I told him I would be going with him to the Ellenville reunion, and that Tandy would be joining us in a few days. I didn't ask him if Gail was going, but he did mention that he had made plans to go with his girlfriend, Cookie.

I sensed something was terribly wrong. When I asked Dad who Cookie was, where he had met her, or did he know her real name, he couldn't tell me. He asked me to call her, saying that her phone number was on the list by his phone. When I looked at the list of telephone numbers, I nearly tore it to shreds. The names of my cousins, Gail, Robert, Beverly, Diane, and Bobbie, and Lee Eakin and Cookie were listed. Conspicuously absent were the names and phone numbers of my mother, my children, and myself. I asked Dad why we weren't on his list. He said he didn't know because Gail had filled it out for him. I found a pen and added our names, then hung our family pictures that I had brought with me on the walls before we left to go to dinner.

It was painfully obvious to me that Gail was still calling the shots, and that Lee was now conspiring with her to try and eliminate our family from my father's life. I was sick to my stomach and could hardly eat, but managed to keep an optimistic front for the sake of my father.

Our conversation was a bit strange. He didn't recall the nursing home, or having been in the hospital, or that my mother had moved to California. He was looking forward to seeing his friends at the Ellenville reunion, but he was a bit sad when he said no one had visited him. I didn't have the heart to tell him the reason he had not had any visitors was because no one knew where he was!

Dad was scheduled for dialysis the next morning, so I told him I'd be back the next afternoon. I could see in his eyes that he didn't want me to leave. I assured him that I was only ten minutes away and would return in the morning.

I phoned Sheri the next day and we arranged to meet at her office that morning and discuss our case. On the way to Sheri's office, I stopped at the local JC Penney and bought Dad a pair of pajamas, slippers, handkerchiefs, underwear, and several decent shirts that didn't have huge tropical prints splattered all over them.

It was difficult to see how much of Dad's personality had changed in the short time he was in Florida. I remembered the laughter and fun our family had experienced when we had been together last Thanksgiving in New York, just over one year ago. Whether it was due to his stroke, the medication he was taking, or the absence of his immediate family, there was definitely something missing in the man I had known as my father. I only hoped Tandy didn't notice the change when she arrived.

The relationship between a father and daughter was one that was stronger than distance, time, or outsiders could ever destroy. The relationship between a grandfather and his grandchildren was ten times that, and more. My husband's father had passed away when Tandy was still a small child, so my dad was the only grandpa she had ever known. From the time she was born, he had been a major part of her life, not only on holidays and special events, but also throughout her twenty-two years. When Gail made the selfish decision to separate my parents, she threatened the very existence of my daughter's relationship with her grandfather, and I was going to do everything a mother could to protect her child.

At Sheri's office, I read through Gail's testimony she had given to the divorce attorney. It was full of lies and vicious attacks on my mother and me. The false accusations were always on the subject of money. I wondered what price she could possibly put on the love of a daughter for her father or a granddaughter for her grandfather.

The next day before the reunion, I met Dad for breakfast. He told me Cookie was going with us because he'd invited her. I thought that was a bit strange since, as far as I knew, Cookie wasn't from Ellenville nor did she know any of Dad's friends, but I was just relieved that Gail had not made an appearance. When Cookie arrived, Dad began acting very strangely. She picked out his suit for the party and helped him dress, buttoning his shirt and even zipping up his pants, although he had been able to do that for himself quite well before she had arrived. He kept referring to her as his girlfriend, but I could tell from Cookie's body language that she was performing these tasks more out of a sense of duty than as a romantic partner.

The party was a lot of fun. Many people were there that I hadn't seen in years, and many inquired about my mother. A few spoke to my dad but didn't stay very long. Only one person asked me about Gail who, as I'd guessed, had planned on being at the reunion until she learned I was in town. I could only assume she had found out because Cookie had told her, since no one else knew I was there, affirming once again that I should trust my instincts.

We sat together, me on Dad's right and Cookie in the seat next to Dad on the opposite side. It was a bit uncomfortable to me since my mother had always occupied the seat on my father's left. Several people stopped by to say hello, but I could tell they were also uncomfortable when they saw a strange woman sitting next to my father. It was obvious Cookie did not belong there and everyone knew it. Meanwhile, Dad was having problems remembering anyone's name, and I could see he was becoming more and more depressed as the afternoon wore on.

The waiter put a tray of desserts on the table. I suggest to Dad that he eat only the sugar-free items because of his diabetes, but he argued with me and ate whatever he wanted, while Cookie sat by and watched. I didn't want to start a fight with so many people around so I changed the subject. I told Dad that Tandy was coming into town the next day and we'd all go out to lunch together, which seemed to cheer him up quite a bit.

I went outside for a cigarette and met Cookie in the parking lot. Since we were alone, I was able to ask her exactly what her relationship to my father was. She said she was a nurse who visited Dad a couple of times a week to take him out to lunch and to Elks meetings. Then she off-handedly mentioned that Gail owed her money and that she didn't know anything about the situation with the guardianship. I didn't feel it was the time to go into personal details; with her connection to Gail, I wasn't about to reveal my true intentions of finding a way to get my dad out of Florida.

We ended up leaving the party early. Dad, who had always been the life of the party, was uncharacteristically tired. We took him back to Sunrise and went to the nurse's office where they checked Dad's vitals, including his blood sugar level, which had been elevated after the sweet desserts he had ingested. The nurse injected the insulin into his stomach and I shut my eyes. Dad had always been diabetic, but he had controlled it with pills. If this was the way the "guardian" was watching over my father, then they were doing a lousy job.

The next day I met Tandy at the airport and we drove to Vic's for an early lunch. Since Dad wouldn't be back from dialysis until later that afternoon, we spent some time shopping in the local mall. It was nice to be with an old friend and my daughter. For a brief time, I was able to relax but it was all-too brief. Tandy and I met Dad later that night and we prepared to go out for dinner, first checking in with the nurse. After testing his blood, the nurse announced that his blood sugar was over four hundred and, according to their procedure, Dad had to go into the hospital. I was furious, but there wasn't anything we could do. The hospital was five minutes away and I offered to drive him, but she refused to allow us to take him ourselves. We had to wait an hour for an ambulance to arrive and transport him to the hospital. Tandy and I arrived at the hospital emergency room where they gave Dad insulin, but the doctors wanted to keep him overnight for observation.

The following day, Tandy and I met with Sheri to plan our next legal action. We made preparations for the hearing on Monday and to call Cookie as a witness, if we could find out her real name.

Later that day, we returned to visit Dad. He looked fine to me but his nurse, Maggie, noticed that the dialysis shunt in his shoulder was becoming infected, so they were going to operate to have it removed and replaced with one in his arm.

I asked if I needed to sign the consent forms as next of kin, but when Maggie checked the records, she informed me that they had no record of any emergency contacts except for Gail Lerner and the guardian, Jewish Family Services. As far as anyone in Florida knew, we did not exist. I gave her my business card and she taped it to the notebook. She also told me that Gail had called, screaming that I was going to kidnap my father. I laughed. Gail would have thought that I would try something like that since she, obviously, would have kidnapped Dad in a New York minute, but I wasn't about to make any move without obtaining legal permission from the court.

Tandy, Dad, and I finally had an opportunity to talk in private without Cookie or the staff at Sunrise lurking around. We discussed his wishes to leave Florida, how much he missed his family, and his desire to come to California. Dad didn't know that I had brought my micro-tape recorder with me and had taped the entire conversation to be used, if necessary, as evidence.

Friday morning when Tandy and I went to pick my dad up from the hospital, we found out that he had already been released and that someone had picked him up. We went back to Sunrise with the intention of taking him out to dinner. The nurse met us and adamantly refused to allow him to leave. She screamed at us, saying she could not let him leave since he'd just returned from the hospital. The fact that he wasn't sick and that she was the one who put him in there in the first place didn't faze her.

My dad was so upset. He had gotten dressed to go out for lunch, and now they wouldn't allow us to leave. I called Neil Newstein, the executive director of Jewish Family Services, and begged him to allow us to take my dad out of the facility for an hour. He flatly refused, saying the decision was at the nurse's discretion. I didn't believe him, but the nurse threatened to call the police if we left with my father. There was nothing we could do. Dad was virtually being held against his will, imprisoned by a Florida guardian who cared little for the "ward" he was legally responsible for.

I continued taking detailed notes, planning to use them at the hearing on Monday.

Defeated for the moment, Tandy and I left—alone. Although my daughter was trying to put on a courageous face, I could see she was having a difficult time holding back her tears. She couldn't understand why these strangers were so set on keeping us apart. I tried to reassure her that once we went to the hearing, the judge would see the truth and everything would be fine. I wasn't as confident as I thought I sounded.

It was 5:30 p.m. when we finally returned to our hotel room. The light was blinking on the phone indicating there was a message. It was Sheri telling me that she had received a call from the court clerk at five minutes to five informing her that the hearing had been cancelled. The courts closed at five, leaving no time at all to petition for an emergency hearing. The trip had been completely in vain.

It was obvious to me that Jewish Family Services had contacted the Shalloway firm, that they realized why we were in Florida, and had cancelled the hearing in order to thwart any attempt on our part to have our day in court. (According to the final accounting report, the conversation to discuss whether the "ward" should be able to leave the facility with family, which was denied, had cost my father $137.50.)

Over the weekend, Tandy met with Dad's court-appointed attorney, David Centola. At first, she thought he would be on our side, but she quickly changed her thinking after their meeting.

Gail's poison had penetrated through to each and every person who encountered my father. It was as though some insidious disease had infected every person who had control over my father's life and his finances.

What was so ironic was that I was the one who "hired" Jewish Family Services to help deal with my cousin, and I had agreed to David Centola's representing my father—but they had all turned against us.

Tandy left for Oklahoma, not knowing if she would ever see her grandfather again. I left for California determined that my father would not be buried in an unmarked Medicaid grave somewhere in Southern Florida.

I vowed that the next time I was sitting on a flight from Florida to California, the person sitting next to me would be my father.

Chapter 12

The events of the past several months were beyond my comprehension. I had agreed initially to have Jewish Family Services appointed as temporary guardianship for my father, with the understanding that they would help free my father and reunite him with our family. After all, what better organization would understand the importance of a Jewish family than one dedicated to *Jewish family services*? Instead, they had become ten times the adversary that I had contacted them to help me defeat.

The Jewish holiday of Passover celebrates Moses leading the Jewish people out of Egypt and into freedom. Over the years, the holiday had become a family tradition where I invited as many as twenty-five friends and family into our home for the *Seder* dinner. My parents would fly in from New York, along with my cousin Bobbie who would join her sisters, my other cousins Diane and Beverly. The entire family, along with Beverly's now deceased husband Vito Scotti, and a few of my close friends would gather round a huge table to eat and sing traditional Passover songs in Hebrew and, some not-so-traditional, in English.

One of the songs recounted Moses' frustration with Pharaoh and the number of plagues inflicted upon the Egyptians due to Pharaoh's stubbornness in denying the Hebrews their freedom to leave Egypt. "Let My People Go" became my own personal theme song with a slight variation on the words: "Go down, Robin, go down to Florida. Tell Lee Eakin to LET MY FATHER GO!"

Although the three hurricanes that hit the southern coast of Florida that year might have been seen as a threat of

Biblical proportions, they did as much to sway the guardian's determination to keep my father "imprisoned" in Florida as the ten plagues inflicted upon Egypt did to persuade the Pharaoh of ancient Egypt to free the slaves.

Our family was quickly losing faith in miracles, until Sheri Hazeltine came up with an idea. She would file a motion and petition the court for permission for Dad to come to California for a one-week visit in March. I quickly agreed and began making plans.

My days were now consumed with preparations for my father's "visit." Without knowing exactly when Dad would be allowed to leave, or if the court would even grant the petition, I went forward with plans for his arrival the third week in March. I had to show proof that Dad's medical needs would be met, with the most important being his dialysis. This was more of a problem than I had anticipated. None of the three dialysis centers in our immediate area had any openings. Without access to a kidney center, it wouldn't be possible for Dad to travel. I made an appointment with the head of the kidney center in Thousand Oaks, which was five minutes from my house. I explained the situation to the head of the facility. Once she heard what was going on in Florida, she set up an emergency schedule for my father, at five o'clock in the morning. I didn't care what time slot she gave him, as long as Dad would be able to be "recycled" once he arrived in California.

The admitting nurse needed Dad's medical information from the guardian in order to complete the paperwork and faxed the request to Jewish Family Services. As I expected, the request was ignored, but we reserved the week of March 20 in anticipation of gaining a positive ruling on our motion.

My next step was to find a place for my father to stay for his visit which, if my plans were successful, would last a great deal longer than one week. As much as I would have loved to have my dad stay in my home, I had no knowledge of testing blood sugar, monitoring blood pressure, or administering insulin. The nurses in Florida had provided my father's medication, and I needed to find a similar facility for him before his arrival. Unfortunately, the medical staff at my mother's Sunrise facility in Westlake, and several other facilities in Thousand Oaks, didn't have the skilled nursing Dad needed.

On the way to class one day, there was an accident on the freeway and traffic was to Santa Rosa Road. Santa Rosa Road ran right by Sunrise Brighton Gardens, an assisted living facility in Camarillo, about ten minutes from my house. To this day, I wonder if that "accident" was just a coincidence, or another small miracle.

The next day I phoned Ted, the residence director of the facility, and we made an appointment for that afternoon. Ted showed me the perfect room for my father on the second floor with a gorgeous mountain view. Having been familiar with the Sunrise procedures, I quickly filled out the paperwork while Ted phoned the Brighton Gardens in Florida and requested that they fax the medical information. He also informed me that since the same company owned both facilities, he would waive the $4,000 registration fee. He also gave me a list of doctors who visited the residents at Sunrise and recommended Dr. Robert Feiss for my father. We phoned Dr. Feiss from Ted's office, made the appointment tentatively for the week of March 20, even though at the time I had no idea whether or not my father would be able to keep the appointment.

Across the parking lot from Brighton Gardens was a Bank of America branch. I needed some cash, so I drove over to the ATM. While I was standing in line, I noticed a young man in Orthodox Jewish attire speaking to a group of people. A sign overhead read "Future Home of Chabbad Jewish Center of Camarillo." I walked over and introduced myself to Rabbi Lang. The two of us went into the Center and I told him the entire ordeal our family was going through. I'm not a very religious person, but in those few minutes, a feeling of peace came over me.

For the first time in months, I felt as if everything was going to work out, that maybe there was a Higher Power who not only parted the Red Sea for hundreds to safely cross to freedom, but also created small miracles in each of our lives to free us from tyranny and lead us to the "promised land." I only knew that we needed one more small miracle: Judge Vonhof's signature on the visitation request.

For the next few days, there wasn't anything else to do but wait. Of course, every plan I had made was under the pretext that my father would only be visiting California for the duration of the visitation. I purchased a round trip ticket for him with no intention of his ever using the return ticket. I even called my cousins Beverly and Diane to arrange for them to visit Dad while he was here that "week." As much as I despised them, I knew they were still in contact with Gail and any hint of my plan not to return him to Florida would get back to her. I wasn't about to take any chances. I knew Gail would report any hint of deception to the guardian, and this would jeopardize my entire plan. I didn't have any problem lying to them.

Dad's "get out of jail" ticket arrived via fax at 7:45 a.m. on Friday, March 18, 2005. Judge Vonhof had signed the Stipulation Agreeing to Ward's Visit to California March 20-27, 2005. The best line on the agreement affirmed that my little "act" had been successful: "The visit is not opposed by any party at this time."

I immediately phoned my dad and told him I was on my way to Florida to take him to California for a week to visit the family. He asked me why it was only for a week, and I told him that was all the time we were given, and that I'd see him Saturday. It was déjà vu all over again. First, I'd flown to New York to bring my mother to California; now it was my father's turn. (I joked with my husband, wasn't he glad I only had two parents?)

With the theme song to *Mission Impossible* running through my head, I packed an overnight bag and headed to Burbank Airport for the "rescue" flight to Florida.

Chapter 13

I phoned Sheri when I arrived at the hotel to let her know I was in Florida. Even though I was aware of attorney-client privilege, I kept her in the dark regarding my true intentions. I had to make certain that I'd covered every detail. One wrong move, one innocent slip of the tongue about what I was about to do, would have resulted in an immediate action by the guardian agency to prevent our departure and possibly cancel the entire trip. Fortunately, it was Friday so their attorney wouldn't be able to file an objection with the court until Monday, and Dad and I would be on a plane headed to the West Coast long before they had a chance. Two could play at this game, and I had become an expert player.

Dad was in dialysis Saturday morning when I arrived at the Sunrise facility. I chatted with the staff about Dad's visit, and what was on their schedule the rest of the month when he "returned." The nurses were very friendly and provided an entire week's worth of Dad's medication, including all the prescriptions and instructions, insulin, and a blood sugar tester. There was no indication that anyone had the slightest clue that my father wasn't ever coming back. To be on the safe side, I phoned Cookie and invited her to Sunday brunch, so even Gail's "spy" would believe that Dad was going to be away for only one week.

As I expected, Dad was very happy to see Cookie. Obviously, she had continued visiting Dad after Tandy and I had left; and, just as obviously, she hadn't mentioned the fact she was being paid by Gail to be Dad's "girlfriend." There's a word for what she was, and it wasn't "caregiver." I kept up the façade throughout lunch. Cookie mentioned some excellent restaurants we would all go to when I brought Dad back to Florida the following week. I smiled and agreed with everything, playing the part to perfection. I was barely able to keep my lunch down.

We returned to Dad's room and I began packing what few clothes he owned. It had to appear as if he were going to return, so I left some articles in the closet. All the tropical print Floridian shirts remained behind. Even though Dad kept saying he never wanted to go back to Florida, I had to remind him the visit was only for a week, in case he gave the impression to any of the staff that he wouldn't be returning.

Monday morning when I arrived to take Dad to the airport, he had a surprise visitor. Jewish Family Services had hired a psychiatrist, who was again begin paid by my father's estate, to examine Dad and determine whether or not he wanted to leave. I was confidant Dad would respond positively, but held my breath during the entire interview process. Dad had some difficulty remembering the name of the President of the United States, but that wasn't unusual for my father even when he was in perfect health! What was more important was that he expressed, in clear and concise sentences, his desire to see his grandchildren and my mother and to spend time with his daughter in California. The interview appeared to be very convincing in our favor, but we didn't have time to find out the official results. I picked up Dad's medications from the nurses' station, gave them a dozen roses as a "thank you" for all their hard work in preparing for Dad's visit, and said we'd see them next week.

Dad and I left for the airport that afternoon. I'd called ahead and arranged for a wheelchair when we arrived, even though Dad didn't want one. The plane was full, and because of the speed of the reservations, Dad was seated in front of me. The woman seated next to him overheard our conversation and offered to trade seats with me. I thanked her profusely and she said, "I hope that if I'm ever in this situation, someone would do the same for me."

I had the window seat. Dad was in the middle, and seated next to him was another very nice young woman who chatted with him the entire flight to Los Angeles. Dad showed her pictures of my daughters, told her how much he was looking forward to seeing them, and said that he never wanted to go back to Florida. Getting Dad out of Florida had been the easy part. Keeping him in California was going to take a lot more effort, and I only had one week to make it happen.

Bill and Michelle, met us at LAX. Michelle hadn't seen her grandfather in nearly two years and their reunion was highly emotional. By the time we arrived home, we were nearly exhausted, but Dad insisted we call my mother to let her know we'd arrived.

Dad spent his first night in California sleeping in his own queen-sized bed, surrounded by his favorite paintings and furniture we had transported from New York when we moved my mother several months before.

Dad was home at last.

Chapter 14

While we were getting Dad settled in at home, I conducted a medical Internet search on the medications he was taking. Once I read the report, my determination to prevent his return to Florida was intensified. Dad had been prescribed Novolin for his diabetes, Lipitor for his cholesterol, Plavix to prevent another stroke, and Phoslo to control phosphate levels because of his kidney failure. All of these medications made sense considering Dad's health issues, but when I looked up the drug Risperdal that Dr. Masserano had prescribed for my father, I nearly had a heart attack of my own. According to the drug company's web site: "Risperdal is an antipsychotic medication used for the treatment of schizophrenia and mania associated with bipolar disorder." My father was not, nor had he ever been, diagnosed with schizophrenia or bipolar disorder. The most frightening information about this drug further stated, "Elderly patients with dementia-related psychosis are at *an increased risk of death* and Risperdal is *not approved for the treatment of patients with Dementia-Related Psychosis.*" In addition, their studies suggest an *increased risk of elevated blood sugar*—and it is sometimes potentially fatal in patients with diabetes!

MY GOD, I thought. If I hadn't rescued Dad from the Florida guardianship, and had he continued taking Risperdal, the "guardian" would have most likely have killed him! Moreover, with their Medicaid plan naming Jewish Family Services as beneficiary, the agency would have "inherited" everything remaining in his estate!

It was time to call in reinforcements.

83.

Having lived in Thousand Oaks for over twelve years, our family was very well known in the community. We had owned a retail stationery store for over seven years, and both Bill and I were very active in politics and the local Chamber of Commerce. Everyone that I asked for help didn't hesitate.

First I phoned the physician who was now Dad's primary doctor, Dr. Feiss. He immediately faxed a letter to Sheri stating that Dad did not want to return to Florida and that due to his dialysis and other medial issues, the trip could be highly dangerous to his health. The bank manager at Washington Mutual set up Dad's checking account. Marian at the California DMV helped Dad obtain his California ID card. My fellow members of Thousand Oaks Elks Lodge #2477 welcomed Dad with open arms, and voted him into our Lodge as an associate member.

The sun was finally shining on our family in California, except for the small dark cloud that continually hung over our heads. At any time, the Florida guardian could petition the Florida court and demand that Dad be returned to Florida. Unless we had the judge's approval to allow him to stay, in spite of everything I had accomplished, I would be forced to use his return trip ticket.

Over the next several weeks, I tried not to think about the possibility of losing my father again. As much as it disgusted me, I allowed my cousins to visit Dad every other weekend so he would have more definite reasons to remain in California. Although they had not so much as made even one phone call to offer any assistance in the process of getting my father out of Florida, they weren't a bit hesitant to enjoy his company while he was here. Of course, neither my mother nor I were ever invited to accompany them on these visits, which wasn't any great surprise to us. My only concern was for Dad's happiness so he wouldn't be persuaded to return to Florida.

With the most difficult tasks completed, I could concentrate on the financial mess the guardian had created. I went online to see the status of Dad's investments. I discovered the guardian had not only changed the address on my parents' stocks, but had cashed a dividend check that was made out to both my parents as joint tenants, without my mother's knowledge or consent.

When I phoned my parents' tax accountant in New York, I was informed that JFS had not only neglected to file Dad's 2004 tax return, but because of the income generated by their liquidation of Dad's IRAs, we were facing a possible tax bill of over $10,000. The IRS didn't care that my father never spent any of the assets or that the investment money had been depleted to pay the guardianship fees. It was considered income, even though my parents had not received one dime of the assets.

I made several phone calls to the Ellenville village and school tax assessor and was told that those taxes hadn't been paid either. Unless they received payments totaling over $5,000, there would be interest penalties attached and we were in danger of losing the house. I immediately sent the payments by next day air.

The funds were running out faster than I had anticipated. If it had not been for my mother's investments, my parents could very easily have lost their house due to the actions of Jewish Family Services. Nearly all the money my parents had saved for their retirement was gone, leaving only Dad's social security monthly payments to provide for his care. Even knowing Dad was in California didn't prevent Jewish Family Services from cashing Dad's social security check and depositing it into their accounts, which they later used to pay their attorney and themselves. Not a penny of Dad's government funds went to him. Even though my father's physical body was in California, his financial blood continued to be drained by the guardian three thousand miles away. Unless the judge ruled otherwise, they would bleed him dry.

June 1, 2005, was Bill's birthday and the anniversary of our engagement. On that day, I received two gifts: news that Beverly and Diane were moving back to New York to be with their sister, and news from Sheri that the petition granting a telephonic hearing in Florida had been granted, so that we would be able to participate via telephone at the proceeding that would decide Dad's ultimate fate.

The hearing was scheduled for June 17 at 10:30 a.m. in Florida, which was 7:30 a.m. local time. I set up the speakerphone in the living room and made coffee while Michelle drove to pick up Dad and bring him to the house. Sheri phoned at 7:00 to be sure we were ready and to tell us that she thought we might be in trouble. She had arrived at the courthouse early and noticed that all of the opposition, Mark Shalloway, Lee Eakin, and even Dad's court-appointed attorney, were huddled in the corner laughing and joking and sounding extremely confident that they would easily win, especially since we weren't present in court.

I told Sheri that Bill, Michelle, and my dad were in the house waiting for the hearing to begin and we were ready. The phone rang, and we held our breath as the telephonic conference began. Knowing we were on speakerphone and everyone in the Florida courtroom would be able to hear anything I said, I literally bit my tongue many times during Mark Shalloway's opening statements. My daughter kept looking at me, hoping I'd be able to contain myself, but the stakes were too high for me to allow my emotions to be overheard although at one point I opened my mouth and let out the loudest silent scream ever heard!

With the speakerphone on its highest level and my tape recorder hooked into the line, we sat in our living room in Thousand Oaks, California, while Judge Vonhof began the proceeding. This is the actual transcript of the hearing in which my father was finally freed from the clutches of the Florida guardian:

Transcript of Telephonic Hearing

15th Circuit Court of Florida

Friday, July 17, 2005

Judge Vonhof: This system is very unique in that once you start talking you cut off all communication from us back to you. I don't know whether we're gonna be ... what's going on this morning. I just want you to basically listen, and if we want something from you, we'll ask some questions, ok?

Robin: That's fine.

Judge Vonhof: OK

Judge Vonhof: All right, what are we doing this morning?

Mark Shalloway: Good morning, Your Honor. Mark Shalloway, attorney for Jewish Family, the guardian over

Rubin Cohen, and I asked that we have a case management conference today, that I intend that we actually take testimony and produce evidence, but on this case that has a lot going on. I'll get right at it. Ok. Essentially Mr. Cohen is over in California now, and we ah ... hear that the latest is that he is interested in staying there, ah ... Jewish Family's philosophy, as the guardian, is that we serve at the of the pleasure of court, and if, ah ... there is terms under the statute, or if somebody else wants to be guardian, we always also look for what is least restrictive so that restoration ... we raise all those things, and in this case, ah ... the matter came before us, just to refresh Your Honor's recollection, adult protective services had some concerns, and we were appointed guardian. During, ah ... there were a number of issues that, ah ... were I guess controverted that have not really been resolved, but I'm not trying to argue that the court should be made aware of all that is going on in this case, so that we have guidance to come to a quick resolution given the fact that the ward is in fact in California and has been there since late March, I believe. Ah ... under a stipulation entered into by all parties, it was a circumstance where prior to that, the pleading showed that the daughter filed a petition to serve as a successor guardian, ah ... we never had a hearing on that and, I guess, ah ... it could have been set, so in the meantime we felt an obligation to continue our fiduciary purposes. There was, however, reports from Ruby while he was here in Palm Beach County that he did not want, ah ... to be around his daughter, legal time tried to discourage that in the court, or rather encourage to establish his wishes, so, what we tried to do is, he expressed a strong desire to be around his grandkids and as I could say were always coming down here so we were agreeable to having him come out there. Rudy has about $30,000 in a guardianship account. That's all the amount we've been able

to marshal. There is a, as you recall, an attorney where
$11,000 fees were awarded with a lot of controverted issues
whether Ruby had capacity to enter into his ah, ah … divorce
lawyer's representation and if the wife wanted it or not. The
significance of the divorce at this point is that we, as
guardians, have not seen any history of financial support, ah
… from wife or daughter for Ruby. That's not saying that
they won't do it; it's just that we've not seen any history of
that. It's now down to thirty grand and I'm not sure if he's in
an assisted living or nursing home or less restrictive, but the
bottom line is we have custody of thirty grand. Ruby had a
marital home in New York. There were a number of other
issues that were part of the discovery in the divorce that were
as far as the divorce action is going, we have an order
verifying the local divorce lawyer's authority to proceed, etc.
but we are simply having to retreat, withdraw as guardian,
what have you, but not seeing anything on either establishing
in California, or any type of hearing to have the daughter
serve as a guardian, as even then it's not the typical, we
welcome the daughter, there's been some concerns about the
daughter. Also, thank you … My take on the course of
dealing with the daughter and council is that ah … there are
pleadings that have been filed as I've said, the hearings have
not been set and conditions that are problematic to try to
resolve these things through just an agreed order and yet
there is a lot of rhetoric. The way this has been the dynamic
of the case in other words, maybe the family of Ruby, the
daughter, the mom, the wife are seeking full restoration. We
don't really feel in a position to support it, because he's been
since March over in California. There have been some things
that are disconcerting to us dealing with the daughter and the
wife in that there have been changes of addresses, to redirect
financial account information over to them without resolving
the underlying issue of … California, restoration down here,

whatever. We just assume sharing financial resources, we want to be of use to Ruby, we don't want to be charging up a bunch of guardianship and attorney's fees on something that ... we are concerned about asking for a voluntary dismissal outright in your case because that might be in another court's jurisdiction to ... Ruby's marital assets. That's where things are at. There maybe something to set up his financial accounts in the future. We want you to be aware that he really isn't here, and that he's not been here, and what your reaction might be and we need you to direct us to file any particular motion. We're not making the best use of Ruby's resources, nor the charity's resources.

Judge Vonhof: Are you there, Robin?

Robin: Yes, we're here.

Judge Vonhof: Who is there with you?

Robin: My father, Ruby, is here; his granddaughter, my daughter Michelle is here; and my husband, William Westmiller is here.

Judge Vonhof: OK

Sheri Hazeltine: It is very early in the morning in California; I believe that's why Mrs. Cohen is not there.

Judge Vonhof: We did an order; we appointed Dr. Kolina, who basically came back and said there should be no restoration, didn't he?

Sheri Hazeltine: Well, I believe that he ... they had him on Risperdal …

Judge Vonhof: Obviously, I no longer have any control over the person, nor do I want to have it if everything is going smoothly. It might turn out that we may be throwing him to the wolves, I don't know, but by the same token, everything seems to be going very well. I got a good report from ... he's doing OK.

Sheri Hazeltine: He was examined by a doctor a few days ago.

Mark Shalloway: We're happy to take an exit cue; we are concerned that we don't have the good will of his next of kin, so I think we seek a protection order as a charity. We have done our own diligence investigation. One doctor who was approached, I think he was a nephrologist, and he rejected it, because he didn't feel comfortable. Another health care provider there had said they were not aware there was a guardianship and the change of address. All of those things individually may be mundane; we just want to make sure, as you said, throwing him to the wolves. Again, I'm not oblivious to the fact he's living in California, and still supposedly subject to this court's jurisdiction, but for us to continue in this mode, it's not a healthy mode. We have concerns that all of this kind of communication, like our report to the court, the main thing is that I feel like we want to respond to, because a restoration petition, or a successor guardian petition, or any of those things, and frankly will be ... against the ward's assets and in this report, frankly the credibility of it is unknown to us. It might be 100%, and so I just wanted to disclose at this conference, that our limitation and knowledge about the ward's welfare. We were told early on that he was too ill to come back, then the latest is that he is very high functioning...

Judge Vonhof: Let me talk to Robin. Robin, where is your dad living right now?

Robin Westmiller: My father is in the Brighton Gardens Sunrise Assisted Living in Camarillo. I sent an email to the Shalloways, with address and phone number, I sent an email to JFS and to Neil Newstein with the information two weeks ago. All of the accounts of the fiduciary are on my computer to the penny. I will be more than happy to fax that to you as to exactly where the monies are. My father had a $93,000 annuity which JFS was transferred to their account by his accountant and as I understand it, there is only $50,000 left on that. We have no accounting on that. I'm also taking care of my mother who is now also living in California and all her fiduciary responsibilities. Again, my father has his own checking account, he has access to his own funds any time he needs it, across the Bank of America from his facility, and he's perfectly capable of going over to the drug store and buying his own products. He's signing himself out. The doctor who was reluctant to sign off on that was his eye doctor. He performed a cardiac, excuse me, a cataract surgery so now my father can read, and he called me and said he wasn't comfortable because he's not a physician, and that was the contention on that. On the other hand, I don't know if the attorneys are aware of the fact that I'm registered with the California State Bar Association as a law student, so everything that's being done is on the up and up, is being done through the legal process, and my father is here with the family very happy. He was with the Chabbad, which is the Orthodox Jewish group out here. He went to a performance last night with the Jewish group. The rabbi is wonderful. He goes to the Elks, and there is no need for my dad to have a guardian. He's perfectly capable, other than the fact we got him up at 6:30 in the morning, and I think you would really… should address some of your questions to my dad; he's sitting right here.

Judge Vonhof: What is the status of the divorce case?

Robin Westmiller: Well, the status is my father, you
can ask him, he never wanted a divorce. This was instigated
by my cousin Gail who instigated everything. She basically
had him in Florida, isolated him from the family for three
months, which is why I called the Florida hot line last July,
because she took him to Attorney Raab's office, signed a
revocation of my mother's power of attorney. She signed it,
her boyfriend co-signed it as witnesses. She received the
power of attorney; she got her name on the accounts. She
tried to cash a check for $50,000. She hid him from us for
three months; we didn't know where he was. Eleanor Parker
interviewed her July of last year and within ten days, signed
the emergency temporary guardianship which was only
supposed to go for sixty days with the understanding in that
petition that he was to be returned to his wife in Ellenville,
but my cousin just went after him, in his state. When I was in
Florida, I found him in the hospital with a shattered shoulder,
an ulcerated heel, and kidney failure, which he did not have
when he left. My name was not on any of the information as
next of kin, and that's when I instituted the emergency phone
call to the Florida hot line. Eleanor suggested JFS. I called
Lee Aikin and explained the situation with the understanding
that this was going to be a temporary emergency in order to
get my cousin Gail out of the family finances. This is all in
the history of what has been going on throughout the year.

Judge Vonhof: Has there been anything done on the
divorce case at all in the recent months?

Robin Westmiller: It was my understanding at the
beginning; they were going to withdraw from the divorce.
That was what Lee said, that is what my father said. My

mother never wanted this divorce. She had to find an attorney to contest it and they never wanted this. My dad's right here; he can tell you. My parents, since they've been out here, have gone out for dinners together; we've had Passover together; they're seeing each other all the time. The reason they're not in the same facility is that the level of care my father needs, which is the dialysis three a week and his sliding scale insulin, the facility that my mother is in does not have that level of care, which is why they're in two different Sunrise facilities.

Judge Vonhof: Rubin, can you hear me, ok?

Rubin Cohen: Yes.

Judge Vonhof: Do you want the divorce case in New York dismissed?

Rubin Cohen: Yes.

Judge Vonhof: Ok, have you had any conversation with the lawyer who filed for you recently?

Rubin Cohen: No.

Judge Vonhof: How's everything going for you?

Rubin Cohen: Pretty good.

Judge Vonhof: Are you feeling OK?

Rubin Cohen: Very much so, yeah.

Judge Vonhof: Everything is all right for you out there?

Rubin Cohen: Yup.

Judge Vonhof: If I do an order that restores your capacity and we close this guardianship down, is that what you want me to do?

Rubin Cohen: Yes.

Judge Vonhof: OK. That's what we're going to do. I'll take you off the phone. I've got some paperwork that I've got to do to make sure we get this thing closed out properly, but we'll be sending out copies of everything that I do and we'll get this thing closed down 'cause you don't need me in your life, I don't think.

Rubin Cohen: No.

Judge Vonhof: OK?

Rubin Cohen: Yes.

Robin Westmiller: Thank you, Your Honor.

I could hardly contain my excitement when I heard Judge Vonhof ask Dad, *"If I do an order that restores your capacity and we close this guardianship down, is that what you want me to do?"* No one in their right mind would have said no, not even someone judged to be incapacitated.

It may have been 8:30 in the morning Pacific Coast time, but we opened a bottle of champagne and celebrated. At the very least, I had been hoping the judge would rule that Dad could remain in California, but to have ruled restoration of Dad's capacity was completely unexpected, not only by my family, but also apparently by everyone in attendance in the Florida courtroom. Sheri called ten minutes later to say she was so ecstatic with the ruling that she was near tears. She also said the opposing attorneys were stunned into silence, which is quite rare for Mark Shalloway, and that their mouths had dropped open when they realized they had lost one of their cash-cow "wards."

After breakfast, we drove Dad back to Sunrise. We had won a major battle in the fight for my father, and the entire staff cheered our triumphant return. Dad was finally free from the threat of being forced to return to Florida. His incapacity status, which should never have been ordered in the first place, had been legally removed. According to the official Order Establishing Procedure, signed on June 20, 2005, the "need for a guardianship no longer existed."

If this were a made-for-television movie, the credits would be rolling over a very happy ending.

Unfortunately, reality is never quite that simple, especially when it comes to money. The court gave the order returning my father's mental capacity, but it was going to take much more than a single telephonic hearing to return the thousands of dollars Jewish Family Services and attorneys Howard Raab and G. Mark Shalloway had effectively stolen from my parents' estate.

We had managed to win a major battle, but the war was far from over.

Chapter 15

There is a word that every first year law student learns to dread. The word has more meanings than the Hebrew word *shalom* and more interpretations than "the meaning of *is*." That word is "reasonable."

The common definition of "reasonable" is "not excessive or extreme; fair," and a "reasonable time" would be a wait time less than or equal to one month. However, when one deals with the law, the "black letter" legal definition is much more complicated. In legal terms, "reasonable time" is defined as "the time needed to do what is required to be done, based on *subjective circumstances*."

For lawyers, "reasonable" time is the amount they need to do everything they can in their own interests before complying with a court order, and "reasonable" compensation is as much as they can get away with in billing "for their services." In our case, "reasonableness" was based on Jewish Family Services and their attorney Shalloway, and Shalloway's subjective interpretation of what was reasonable; especially when it came to draining whatever might be remaining in my father's account, even after he was no longer under their control. In this case the guardian agency was free to interpret the court order to "file a final accounting of all of their activities regarding the finances of the ward within a reasonable time" to mean they had all the time in the world to continue to charge fees and deduct as much as they could from whatever was left in my father's accounts before filing their "final" accounting report.

Instead of closing the file on June 20, 2005, or shortly after the date the guardianship was effectively over,

Shalloway and Shalloway continued to charge for every fax, every phone call, and even $150 for travel to and from the court hearing. Under the law, the word "final" does not necessarily mean the end. The first "final" report was filed on July 29, 2005. The remaining assets at that time in my father's joint account held in the Jewish Family Services name, was only $30,364.52 from over $257,000! Meanwhile, the taxes were due on my parents' New York property, both the rents on the Sunrise facilities my parents were now living in were coming due; and, because JFS had failed to withhold any taxes from the liquidation of my father's IRA accounts, we were looking at an income tax bill of close to $10,000. The amount left in my dad's account was just about enough to cover the expenses, but at least we would have the check in hand in a few weeks—or so we thought.

It had been over two months since the judge's order restoring my dad's capacity and ordering JFS to return whatever monies were left to the ward, and I began to realize that what a "reasonable person" understands to be the definition of "reasonable time," and what attorneys believe it to be is a totally different interpretation. It was the end of August, and the check still hadn't arrived.

What did arrive, however, was a little hurricane called Katrina.

Hurricanes throughout September, and the Jewish High Holy Days of Rosh Hashanah and Yom Kippur in October 2005 continued to delay the reimbursement of my father's funds. I expected to see a check arrive the first of November, but again no check arrived.

What did arrive were more "final" reports. An "Amended" Final report arrived on September 2005 a "Supplemental" Final report on November 17, 2005, and yet another "Amended Supplemental" Final report was filed on January 5, 2006 after the guardian agency and their attorney deducted $8,348.50 in additional guardianship and attorney fees, probably to pay themselves for filing all the "final" reports!

The first week of December, I received a phone call from Sheri informing me that she had received a phone call from Kristin E. Miller, the guardianship case manager from the law offices of Shalloway and Shalloway. Kristin said Dad's account was closed and they would be sending the check. I didn't know if I was more surprised by the additional amount the attorneys and Jewish Family Services had taken, or the fact they had left any money at all in Dad's account.

What I did find surprising was the "extortion" letter which accompanied the check, stating that Sheri was to deposit the check into an escrow account and hold it until my father signed a waiver stating that he "waives all objections, and consents to the disbursements and distributions proposed" and "releases the guardian from all further liability in connection with above-styled guardianship."

Being an attorney with integrity, Sheri mailed the check to me along with the waivers. Being someone who wasn't about to have my father sign away his legal right to seek retribution, we declined the "invitation" to sign the waiver and immediately deposited the check into Dad's account. I paid the Sunrise bill, property taxes, and income tax bills.

With what little that was left, I took my parents out to dinner to celebrate what we thought was the "final" end to the Florida fiasco.

Under normal circumstances, this would have been the end of the story, but nothing that had occurred over the past eighteen months was "normal," especially when dealing with an unscrupulous "guardian" and their high-power attorneys. While visiting my father on April 7, 2006 I went to his room and found an envelope lying by his bed containing the Petition for Discharge of Guardian stating we only had thirty days from the date of service to file objections. The papers had been mailed to my father's facility, and signed for by the receptionist on March 17, 2005. Neither Sheri nor I had received a copy. Had I not found them when I did, the thirty days would have expired. I immediately sent Sheri an *urgent* email and she filed for a thirty-day extension on April 13, 2006.

As of the date of this writing, I have no idea if we'll ever be able to recover the thousands of dollars squandered away while Dad was a ward of Jewish Family Services, especially since the members of the Board of Directors of Jewish Family Services are unaware of the devastation their organization inflicted on our family, nor do they seem to care.

I contacted a member of the Board of Director of Jewish Family Services, Ron Kauffman, the host/producer of Senior LifeStyles Intelligent Talk Radio, Inc. News Radio, 1290 WJNO, in West Palm Beach. He responded to my request to appear on his program with a short and very curt response: "Thanks for the offer, but I'll pass. While you are correct in noting that I serve on the Board of Directors at Jewish Family and Children's Services, I am *not familiar with your case or personal situation* and I prefer not to involve my program with issues that are personal." If a member of the board of directors of this agency does not wish to *become involved*, then this type of abuse will continue to be perpetuated for many years to come.

The financial loss to our family was an epic tragedy, but one with a happy ending. My cousins Beverly and Diane moved back to New York. Neither they, Gail, Norman, nor Robert have any contact with my father. My mother's health has improved to the point that she was able to move out of the assisted-living facility and is now in her own two-bedroom home in Leisure Village across the street from my father's Sunrise Assistant Living Facility. They are both only ten minutes from my home and my children can spend time with their grandfather without any restrictions.

For the first time in two years, our family celebrated Thanksgiving together. We had a great deal to be thankful for. In January of 2006, we were featured on NBC Nightly News on the subject of the "sandwich" generation.

This Passover, I felt more a part of the struggle and victory our People experienced when they were at last free from Pharaoh's tyranny. They were forced from their homes, taking what little they could carry, and went on to the Promised Land.

In our case, our freedom did not lead my father to Canaan, but to a land flowing with sunshine, beaches, and mountains: Camarillo, California.

My parents left behind a lifetime of material possessions in New York. However, they can now look forward to a new life together, surrounded by all the very precious things that money can't buy: the love of a daughter for her father, the love of grandchildren for their grandparents, and the love of two people who can live out the rest of their lives knowing no one—not a cousin, or a judge, or even the entire Florida State Guardianship System—will ever be able to control, manipulate, or threaten them again.

I am Ruby's DAUGHTER from the bakery. I have his freckles. I have his blue eyes and we share the same O-negative blood. And blood, sometimes, *is* thicker and stronger than water or anything else—but it still tastes lousy with scotch.

Epilogue

On June 26, 2007 my father passed away in Thousand Oaks, California at the age of 84. There was no life insurance, no assets left in any of his accounts. He was with his family, myself, my mother and my three daughters. On November 20, 2008, my mother Reginia Cohen passed away, also in Thousand Oaks, four days after her 84th birthday. Due to the enormous stress of having lost her husband, her home and everything they had shared over the years, her weight had dropped from 125 to 79 pounds. I have no doubt that the people involved with these events were directly responsible for both of my parent's deaths.

After becoming more involved with the guardianship abuse issue nationwide, I've come to the conclusion that there is no justice for victims or their families. "Wards" have fewer rights than serial killers. As our population ages, abuses such as what was perpetrated on our family will continue as long at the courts, the judges, the attorneys and the guardianship system, as it is now, is allowed to violate basic constitutional rights and laws.

The attorney who had promised to represent our estate was suspended for 90 days. During that time, the defense council was able to win a motion to remove me as a representative and substituted another attorney who decided, since he wasn't going to be paid, to file a motion to dismiss. After nearly four years of pursuing justice for our family, it was over.

My application to practice law in California was denied by the California State Bar Association. At the "informal" hearing to discuss my "moral character", they asked me questions specifically about this case and my involvement with the guardianship issue in general. I have no doubt they had already knew the answers.

To this day, I am still being asked to speak to elder abuse organizations and give interviews, if only to spread the word about this very dark secret which public and private guardians, lawyers and judges are hiding from an unsuspecting public. There have been a few guardians who have lost their licenses; some have even gone to jail, but like weeds, when one is eradicated, thousands more pop-up to take their place.

One warning I hope the readers of this book will take to heart;

DO NOT GIVE MONEY TO AN ORGANIZATION WHO OFFERS TO HELP!

There are many scammers out there with fancy websites and bogus blogs who may look legitimate and some have even filed for non-profit status, but if they ask for donations, DO NOT GIVE THEM ANYTHING! They have no intention of using that money for any other purpose other then their own! Money won't solve this problem when it's money that is causing this problem in the first place.

The nightmare of guardianship abuse has been going on for more than 30 years and will most likely go on for another 30 or more. Our family has suffered, but we're on the road to recovery.

It is my sincere hope that those who read about our family's nightmare will gain some insight into what can happen before it's too late.